Advance praise for *Don't Oil the Squeaky Wheel*

Tells you what you need to know to win in the game of leadership in these turbulent times.

—J. W. Marriott, Jr., Chairman of the Board and President
Marriott International, Inc.

This is a motivating and inspirational read—it takes us back to the basics—reminding all leaders that true excellence is only achieved through their people.

—Carol Wilson, Chief Information Officer
SAP AG, Germany

An easy-to-read and entertaining book which will give you lots of powerful advice on how to improve as a business leader. Dr. Rinke presents his ideas in a simple and straightforward fashion—yet, practicing what Wolf preaches can make a radical difference in your life.

—Jesper Moeller, Executive Vice President
External Affairs & Human Capital
ISS A/S, Denmark

Wolf Rinke knows how to have fun and entertain you while providing valuable tools and resources to improve your leadership skills.

—Thomas L. Phillips, Chairman and President
Phillips International, Inc.

Not getting the results you want from your people? This book can save you lots of time, money, and aggravation!

—Diana Booher, author
*Speak with Confidence, From Contact
to Contact,* and *Your Signature Life*

Cutting edge! The wisdom and inspiration of Tom Peters and Stephen Covey all rolled into one. Truly a must read. I plan to give a copy of this book to every one of my managers.

—Mark Vengroff, CEO
Vengroff, Williams & Associates, Inc.

This book is a great toolbox to turn your company into an entrepreneurial, empowered culture that provides every team member with a license to act.

—Gudrun Bjorno, Vice President Corporate Education
ISS/AS, Denmark

Don't Oil
the Squeaky Wheel

Also by Wolf J. Rinke, Ph.D.

Winning Management: 6 Fail-Safe Strategies for Building High Performance Organizations, 1997

The 6 Success Strategies for Winning at Life, Love and Business, 1996

Make It a Winning Life: Success Strategies for Life, Love and Business, 1992

The Winning Foodservice Manager: Strategies for Doing More with Less, first edition, 1989, second edition, 1990

Don't Oil the Squeaky Wheel

and 19 Other Contrarian Ways to Improve Your Leadership Effectiveness

Wolf J. Rinke, Ph.D.

McGraw-Hill

New York   Chicago   San Francisco   Lisbon   London
Madrid   Mexico City   Milan   New Delhi   San Juan
Seoul   Singapore   Sydney   Toronto

1 2 3 4 5 6 7 8 9 0   AGM/AGM   0 9 8 7 6 5 4

ISBN 0-07-142993-X

This publication is designed to provide accurate and authoritative information in regard to the subject matter covered. It is sold with the understanding that the publisher is not engaged in rendering legal, accounting, or other professional service. If legal advice or other expert assistance is required, the services of a competent professional person should be sought.

—From a declaration of principles jointly adopted by a committee of the American Bar Association and a committee of publishers.

McGraw-Hill books are available at special quantity discounts to use as premiums and sales promotions, or for use in corporate training programs. For more information, please write to the Director of Special Sales, McGraw-Hill Professional, Two Penn Plaza, New York, NY 10121-2298. Or contact your local bookstore.

Library of Congress Cataloging-in-Publication Data

Rinke, Wolf J.
    Don't oil the squeaky wheel : and 19 other contrarian ways to improve your
    leadership effectivness / by Wolf Rinke.— 1st ed.
        p.   cm.
    ISBN 0-07-142993-X (alk. paper)
    1. Leadership.   2. Management.   I. Title.
    HD57.7.R56   2004
    658.4'092—dc22

                                                                    2004001377

Dedicated to leaders who have
the guts to look at what others do
and do something different.

Contents

Acknowledgments

THIS BOOK WOULD NOT HAVE BEEN POSSIBLE without *you*—my students, clients, audience members, mentees, and the many other people whom I've had the privilege to serve and who have taught me so much. Although I may not be able to acknowledge you by name, I believe that you will find yourself and your wisdom in these pages. So please read on and keep looking for *your* story among these pages.

There are, however, several people to whom I owe a monumental debt of gratitude. They are my unsung heroes—the people who have influenced me more than anyone else.

First and foremost on that list is Marcela, my "Superwoman" and life partner of over three decades and my business partner for over 16 years. I've shared with untold audiences all over the world that Marcela is responsible for 85 percent of my success, and the longer I'm married to her, the more I realize that that percentage may be too conservative. She is the most positive, exciting, and generous person I've ever met who continues to love me unconditionally. I don't know how you do it, Marcela, but please don't ever stop.

I also would like to acknowledge my parents, Horst and Anna, who have instilled the discipline in me that made writing this book possible, who continue to live in harmony with their environment, and who have mastered the art of doing more with less. Hang in there, Mom and Dad; I still have much I want to learn from you.

I acknowledge one of my most ardent "teachers," my youngest daughter, Nicole, who was born with a contrarian gene. I'm fond of telling my audiences that she is responsible for 80 percent of my gray hair and that she does not understand the word *no*, never has and never will. Any time you say no to Nicole, she responds: "I obviously have not given you enough information." This tenacity has served her well in her role as a public interest environmental lawyer who is dedicated to protecting the less fortunate. She is one of those unique people in the world who has a built-in moral compass that compels her to do the "right thing" even if it is at her own expense. In short, in many ways Nicole is everything I've always wanted to be, so whatever you do, Nicole, don't let the "big guys" get you down, and keep doing the right thing.

I also acknowledge my oldest daughter, Jeselle, who is a sales professional who has the ability to sell snow to the Eskimos and have them love it. She is one of the most energetic and motivated individuals anyone could hope to have on their team. I'm truly blessed to have a daughter who has mastered the art of consistently giving 111 percent. Keep up the good work, Jeselle, delivering value to your customers so that they continue to want to buy what you have to sell.

Thanks go to my editor, Barry Neville, for "discovering" me and to all the wonderful folks at McGraw-Hill for helping me transform this book into a "masterpiece" of which I am truly proud.

A thousand thanks to all of you!

About the Author

Wolf J. Rinke, LTC (ret), Ph.D., C.S.P., is a management consultant, keynote speaker, seminar leader, executive coach, and author.

Dr. Rinke, America's business success coach, is the president and founder of Wolf Rinke Associates, Inc., a human resources development and management consulting company. Since 1988 his firm has been *custom* designing and delivering stimulating and informative keynote presentations, interactive problem-solving *"fun*shops," and highly effective consulting, coaching, and educational services. The firm specializes in building high-performance organizations, facilitating trust-building initiatives, providing one-on-one executive coaching, building high-performance teams, and implementing exceptional quality service (EQS) systems.

Dr. Rinke is

- A highly effective management consultant and executive coach with over 30 years of hands-on management and leadership experience.
- A dynamic certified speaking professional (CSP*) who is known internationally for his ability to energize, entertain, and empower. He has spoken to over 80,000 people in 13 countries.

*CSP—a credential earned by fewer than 400 individuals worldwide.

- A widely published author of numerous audio and video programs, hundreds of articles, and 13 books, many of which have been translated into several languages.
- An editor of the electronic newsletters *The Winning Manager: Putting People First* and *Make It a Winning Life: Strategies to Help You Succeed Faster.*
- A media personality who has appeared on hundreds of TV and radio shows.
- A highly decorated retired Lt. Colonel of the U.S. Army Medical Specialist Corps.
- A self-made millionaire who started to work full-time on a ship at age 14.

Dr. Rinke's clients include ACE USA, ARAMARK, Am Red Cross, BCE Emergis (Canada), bil-jax, Bristol-Myers Squibb, Brookings Institution, Cigna, Delta Air Lines, Dept of Health & Human Services, Dole, Duke Power, EAC (Singapore), Giant TMC (Malaysia), ISS A/S (Denmark), Litton PRC, Manor Care, Marriott, MBNA, Michelin, Motorola, NORTEL, OPM, Perez Companc (Argentina), Phillips Publishing, Pierce Leahy, SAP (Germany and United States), Sargento Foods, Select Service Partner (Denmark), Seneca Foods, ServiceMaster, Sinar Mas Group (Indonesia), Sodexho, Sysco, US Foodservice, Warner Bros., and Wyeth-Ayerst, plus hundreds of other companies, organizations, and associations throughout North and South America, Europe, and the Pacific Rim.

To get in touch with Dr. Rinke, contact

Wolf Rinke Associates, Inc.
P. O. Box 350
Clarksville, MD 21029
Phone: (410) 531-9280; fax: (410) 531-9282
WolfRinke@aol.com
www.WolfRinke.com

Don't Oil
the Squeaky Wheel

Knowledge Is *Not* Power

Genius, like a thunderstorm, comes up against the wind.
—SØREN AABYE KIERKEGAARD

KNOWLEDGE IS POWER. How many of you agree with this statement? This is what I like to ask my audience members. And guess what, virtually all hands go up. (I bet you agreed too?) I don't! Here is why. The number of leaders and managers I have had the opportunity to work with who *know* how to lead people always startles me. Some know more than I do. They've got it all together. They can talk a great game, and yet, when I watch what they actually do, which is what consultants and coaches do, I find that generally they do not act in accordance with what they know. They act in accordance with their habit patterns, which typically are based on what has worked for them in the past. The problem—need I say it?—is that we live in a hyperspeeded global economy where what has worked in the past may no longer provide you with optimal results *today*. This is why I wrote this book. It's all about breaking your tried-and-true *Weltanschauung*— your view of the world of leadership—assumptions that have worked for you in the past that need to be revisited, reevaluated, and maybe even, horror of horrors, changed.

Here is the brutal fact: You know an awful lot of stuff. And you are about ready to learn additional cutting-edge strategies from this book—great stuff, stuff that has the potential to change the way you lead people and have an immediate payoff on the bottom line. However, all this out-of-the-box stuff in this book won't do you any good whatsoever *unless you apply* what you have learned and develop powerful *new* habit patterns. (You're familiar with the old saw: If you do what you've always done, you will always get what you've always got. And if you want something different to happen without making a change, that's defined as insanity.) You see, it is not what you know that makes a difference; it's what you do and what you apply over and over again until it causes you to transform new knowledge into a new autopilot response pattern. And this will *not* happen from *reading* this book. (You can read all the diet books in the world and never lose a pound.)

A good example, recently shared with me by Walter, one of my "coachees" (the people I coach) involves one of Walter's grade-school buddies walking up to the high diving board at the beginning of the swimming season and without a moment's hesitation jumping into the pool. Never mind that the dive looked absolutely atrocious. Once he was in the water, the boy floundered so badly that the lifeguards had to pull him out. Once back in the showers, Walter asked his friend what had happened. "Not sure," he said. "Actually, I had it all figured out. I've been reading several how-to-swim books all winter long. But once I hit the water, it just didn't seem to work."

Okay pessimist, I hear your questions: What if the stuff in this book does not work? What if it fails? What if it causes you to fail? First, and let me be a bit emphatic here, *there are no failures;* there are only *outcomes*. If you apply something from this book and it does not give you the results expected, try it again. And if it is really important to you, try it yet again. And if it is superimportant, try it up to seven times. (Lots of things that happen are caused by random events and have nothing to do with the intervention, especially since you are in the people business and people are quite unpredictable.) And if it still does not work, you've learned something you didn't know before—I don't call that failure. On the other hand, if it does work, you've hit the mother lode—a new strategy that will enable you to improve your performance, productivity, and maybe even your organization's profitability. (Hey, even I'm getting excited.) The key, then, is not knowledge but doing, experimenting, making yourself uncomfortable—oh, oh, that's a dreadful thought.

And because the doing is so important, this book is very light on theory and very heavy on action. I've even provided you with easily implementable and specific "Smart Steps" at the end of most chapters so that you can apply what you have learned immediately and achieve powerful results *now*.

Lighten Up

Oh, and one more thing: I also would like you to have fun while reading this book. Why? Because—and this is important, so take note—*if it's fun, it gets done*. But you protest, "We've got work to do; we don't have time to have fun." Think again. According to serious research conducted for more than four decades and reported in the prestigious *Harvard Business Review*, executives who are witty—are you ready for this—"get bigger bonuses and better performance ratings." Why? Because "Humor, used skillfully, reduces hostility, deflects criticism, relieves tension, improves morale, and helps communicate difficult messages."[1] So quit taking yourself and your work so seriously, and lighten up. One of the best ways to do this is to laugh at yourself. Just in case you find this a bit difficult, I've provided you with an opportunity to "Smile" at the end of each chapter. (Remember, you don't have to exercise all your funny bones, just the ones you want to keep.)

So get ready, get set, and let's embark on a journey of discovery, learning, failing, laughing, and building powerful new habit patterns.

Smile

Take advantage of this "new" invention. *BOOK* is a revolutionary breakthrough in technology. It has no wires, no circuits, and no memory chips. It requires no external source of power and no monitor, keyboard, or mouse to operate. There is nothing to be plugged in or turned on. It's so easy to use that even a five-year-old can operate it. It's compact, portable, and self-contained and can be used anywhere—in the bathroom, in bed, and even snuggling up by a crackling fire in your favorite chair.

This technological marvel is constructed of sequentially numbered sheets of paper, and each is capable of holding thousands of bits of information. The pages are manufactured using a unique technology called a *binding* that keeps the pages in their correct order. Using a process called *double-sided technology* (DST) allows manufacturers to use both sides of the paper, thereby increasing the information density, reducing weight, and minimizing costs below that of a modest dinner in an inexpensive restaurant. Best of all, manufacturers are able to achieve an almost unlimited increase in information density simply by using more pages.

BOOK requires no special storage device and never gets infected by viruses or worms. It never crashes or requires rebooting, and it is always on, to be used any place, any time, simply by opening it. Users scan each page optically to download the information directly into their "hard drive." To progress through *BOOK*, the user simply flicks a finger. The browse feature allows the user to move instantly from page to page and even go forward and backward. The higher-priced models feature an optional device called an *INDEX* that allows the user to instantly find the exact location of specific information. During interruptions, the user merely closes *BOOK* and can restart *BOOK* at the exact same location with another optional device referred to as a *BOOKMARK*, or users who are minimalist can achieve the same results by employing a simple technique referred to as *crimping*.

BOOK has a virtually unlimited shelf life and may be stored with other units without any interference or special technological devices.

One other unique feature is that the user can customize *BOOK* by making notes in the margins using an optional programming system referred to as *portable enhancing notation styluses (PENS)*. Best of all, *BOOK* may be shared with an unlimited number of users without paying any additional licensing fees, and to the delight of even the most ardent environmentalist, *BOOK* is totally recyclable.

SMART STEPS

Get rid of "ya-but." I hear this all the time: "That's very interesting, but. . . . " Avoid the "ya-buts" and other idea-killing phrases such as "This will never work for me" or "This is all fine in theory, but. . . ." Every time you say "ya-but," you have opened an escape hatch for yourself. Remember the last time your boss paid you a compliment such as, "I appreciate you finishing this project on time, but. . . ." That's right, you didn't hear the compliment. All you heard was what came after the *but*. (That was your boss's escape hatch; what came after *but* is really what she meant to tell you. The rest was just filler to soften the blow. So take your *but* out of your mouth—get it?—and just do it.

Practice, practice, practice! Practice your new skills repeatedly until you have developed a powerful new habit. (You already know why.) Consider your team members, your boss, your dog, and anyone else you interact with on a regular basis as your "laboratory." Keep trying out new strategies to see what results you get.

Just do it. Avoid saying to yourself, "I know this already" or "I have heard this before." You probably have, but are you doing it? When it comes to human behavior, there is very little that's new. What makes it new is when you translate new stuff into a change in your behavior. Now that is magic!

Don't squander your mental energy. At any one nanosecond your mind can have only one thought. That thought can be positive and improve your leadership skills. It can be neutral and keep you where you are. Or it can be negative and take away from your ability to become a highly effective contrarian leader. Oh, while we're at it, also don't squander an iota of your brain power on proving to me that I don't have all the answers—I don't!

Get selfish. Pass what works for you onto your team members, your boss, your customers, your loved ones, and anyone else who might benefit. When you teach someone else, you download your new knowledge into your "hard drive," and it will stay with you forever. Now that's selfish!

Smile. Or better yet, *make* yourself laugh! Once you get the hang of this, you will be well on your way to becoming a highly effective contrarian leader.

Management and Leadership Theories Do Not Work

Leadership is not magnetic personality—that can just as well be a glib tongue. It is not "making friends and influencing people"—that is flattery. Leadership is lifting a person's vision to high sights, the raising of a person's performance to a higher standard, the building of a personality beyond its normal limitations.

—PETER F. DRUCKER

WHEN IT COMES TO MANAGEMENT and leadership there are no "silver bullets." Just look at what happened to management by objectives (MBO), participative management (PM), total quality management (TQM), downsizing, rightsizing, reengineering, and the latest, Six Sigma. For the most part, they did not work. Nohria and colleagues, in a major study of what *does* work, found that "most of the management tools and techniques we studied had no direct causal relationship to superior business performance."[1] Based on what I have learned from my clients, most interventions provide disappointing results for two major reasons.

The first, as I explained in my book *Winning Management: 6 Fail-Safe Strategies for Building High-Performance Organizations,*[2] is because managers have not built a solid *foundation*. Here is what I mean. Let's say that you want to build your dream house, so you buy the best of everything—the best lumber, the best bricks, the best roof, and so on. Then you proceed to build your dream house on *quicksand*. Will it last? Does it matter that you bought the best of everything? Of course not! However, that is how most managers go about building their organizations. They buy the best, or at least the latest, of everything and begin the implementation without a solid foundation, without getting their own heads screwed on right, without changing their basic belief system (especially as it relates to people), without clearly defining their philosophy and core values, and without changing the organizational culture. As a result, just like the dream house built on quicksand, the management model will work for a while, but then it will crumble or even implode. The result is that instead of building a high-performance organization, employees feel used or even abused; they become cynical and strengthen their basic defense mechanisms so that they can remain sane. The outcome is lowered performance and productivity and resistant employees who have mastered the art of playing the "let's pretend" game, who have hardened their protective shells just a little bit more so that they can survive the next management "solution" that will be coming along very soon.

The second reason that management models fail is that U.S. managers are too impatient. (This is an understatement.) They want results yesterday. It reminds me of the person who has been overeating for 30 years and one day steps on the scale only to realize, "I'm fat." He immediately begins his search for a magical diet and, having found it, goes on it right away. And if that diet does not work in 30 days, it is "No good," and the search for another "magic bullet" starts all over again. Effective long-term changes in weight can come about only as a result of a change in *behavior*. And changing one's behavior, as any mental health professional will tell you, takes time—lots of time. Changing the behavior of many people, which is what management models attempt to do, takes even longer—at least three to seven years. (Read that again!) Of course, during that time, several "new" management (dare I say the *F* word?) *fads* come along, which cause managers to jump ship. After all, it's tough to stick with an "outdated" management model when all your colleagues and competitors are doing the "in thing."

In short, what I'm saying is—please listen up because this is a big one—that just about any management or leadership model works *if* you build a strong foundation and *if* you have the guts to *stick with it over the long term*.

Of course, the next question is, What should I stick with? The answer, at least as it relates to building your business, is get back to basics, as demonstrated in a powerful multiyear study of more than 200 management practices applied in 160 companies in over 10 years. The study shoots a whole bunch of sacred cows and identifies what practices *do* produce superior results.[3] Nohria and colleagues found that companies that outperformed their industry peers—they called them "winners"—rigorously practiced four basic, somewhat nonsexy, management practices:

Primary practice 1: Strategy. Identify and practice a clear and focused strategy based on market needs that are consistently communicated to employees, customers, and shareholders.

Primary practice 2: Execution. Be totally committed to disciplined operational execution.

Primary practice 3: Culture. Build and maintain a high-performance-based ethical culture.

Primary practice 4: Structure. Design and maintain a flat, flexible, and fast organizational structure.

In addition, the researchers found that the winning companies supplemented their relentless practice of the four basic strategies with any two of the following secondary strategies. And surprisingly, it did not matter which two they excelled in, nor did it give companies a competitive advantage if they excelled in more than two. So pick two of the following and get on with it.

Secondary practice 1: Talent. Aggressively recruit and retain talented employees.

Secondary practice 2: Innovation. Develop industry-changing products and services and internal improvements.

Secondary practice 3: Leadership. Find and develop leaders with excellent people skills and the ability to anticipate opportunities and solve problems.

Secondary practice 4: Mergers and partnerships. Supplement growth with relatively small mergers and partnerships that support your core business.

The power of this research is that "a company who consistently follows this [4 + 2] formula has a better than 90 percent chance of sustaining superior business performance."[4] So what are you waiting for, start practicing the smart steps that follow and increase your chance of achieving dramatic improvements in performance and productivity.

Smile

We trained hard . . . but it seemed that every time we were beginning to form up into teams we would be reorganized. . . . I was to learn later in life that we tend to meet any new situation by reorganizing; and a wonderful method it can be for creating the illusion of progress while producing confusion, inefficiency, and demoralization. [Please note the date.]

—PETRONIUS ARBITER (FIRST CENTURY A.D.)

SMART STEPS

Stick with any new leadership or management model for at least three years.

Starting this month, build a business strategy that is based on your customers' needs and is focused on your core business.

Aggressively communicate your strategy to your employees, customers, and all other stakeholders.

Push all decision making down to the lowest level so that team members can respond to customer needs.

Set a goal to eliminate all forms of waste to achieve productivity improvements of 5 percent per quarter until you are the most productive in your industry.

Talk less; execute more.

If in doubt, do the right thing. (More about this later.)

Establish a compensation system that ties external and internal rewards to performance (More about this in Chapter 7.)

During the next three months, conduct an employee satisfaction survey and then act on the findings. Repeat this process at least once a year. If you need help, consult the Gallup Organization. It has a great employee satisfaction survey, consisting of only 12 questions, hence known as Q12.[5]

During the next 12 months, reduce the layers of management so that you have no more than five layers between the front-line employee and the senior leader of the organization.

Be Selfish

No man is fit to command another that cannot command himself.

—WILLIAM PENN

"HI, MY NAME IS KEVIN, and I have a need to be liked." This is the story of one of the executives I have coached. And it illustrates vividly why you have to be very selfish and start with number one if you want to be an effective *contrarian leader*.

Kevin was the founder and president of a fast-growing entrepreneurial company that he literally grew from nothing to around $200 million in sales and 160 employees in about 18 years. Because of its explosive growth, Kevin decided that he needed to hire an executive team of five managers to help him manage the company and take it to the next level. For some reason or another, though, very few of the new managers lived up to Kevin's expectations. They either were too aggressive, too slow, too dependent, or didn't work hard enough—and the list goes on. As a result, the new management team was disillusioned, dissatisfied, and demoralized, and Kevin couldn't figure out what *their* problem was. I was brought in as a consultant to straighten out the mess and quickly discovered that it had less to do with the new management team—true, not all were the right fit—and much more with Kevin. Kevin was just not okay inside his own skin, which prevented him from making the hard decisions that would cause others to dislike him. This, in turn, prevented him from holding his team members accountable—you can't give away what you don't have—and from making unpopular decisions, which were required in order to grow the company. (For example, two of the new managers were not the right fit, and several others who had helped build the company had outgrown the company and needed to be asked to leave.) This need-to-be-liked issue prevented Kevin from doing the right thing for the company. And everything—as you can well imagine—went downhill from there.

The moral of this story: If you want to serve as a contrarian leader, you have to be selfish and work on number one first. For example, in this case, Kevin had to discover internal mechanisms that would enable him to like himself so that he would have a lesser need to have himself validated *externally*. (If you are like Kevin, remember that your goal should be to be *respected,* not necessarily liked, because many decisions that effective leaders need to make may be very unpopular with at least some of the people.) In other words, you've got to get your own head screwed on right first before you can help anyone else be a great follower. And it is the followers who are responsible for 85 percent of *your* success. So let's start by looking at the specific foundational habits you must develop if you want to be an effective contrarian leader. (Heads up: These also will make you a more effective spouse, parent, lover, and so on, so read these carefully. Better yet, start working on these right *now.*)

Know Thyself

This has been around since the beginning of time. However, self-awareness without a doubt is the most important leadership attribute. Without it, the other skills won't do you much good. Unfortunately, it is very difficult to develop a keen awareness of your own feelings and emotions. After all, we create the "reality" that we want, and whatever does not align with our reality we distort or treat as exceptions. In other words, we all see and hear what we want to see and hear, even when it does not serve us well. Highly effective contrarian leaders are acutely aware of their own feelings and emotions, as well as their strengths and weaknesses, and are able to tune into those feelings and deal with them in a nondefensive and constructive manner. They are also keenly aware of how their moods and emotions affect others. (To get greater insight into how to sharpen this elusive skill, you may wish to read *Make It a Winning Life: Success Strategies for Life, Love and Business.*[1])

Take Ownership

Tuning into your own emotions is tough to do. Of course, it is even more difficult to take ownership of your feelings. (That employee is worthless. The customers are a big pain. The chief financial officer got me really upset—enough said?) And without ownership, nothing—yes, I do mean nothing—will change! Taking responsibility for everything that is going on in your organization allows you to choose a more constructive emotional response. Managing yourself means that you've developed the ability to deal with the leaderships' ups and downs—but especially the downs—in a constructive and positive manner by "reframing" and by interrupting "triggers" that take you on a downward spiral. Leaders who have not mastered this skill are frequently depressed, worry incessantly, and suffer from seemingly insurmountable obstacles and stressors. On the other hand, those who know how to manage their emotions experience just as many "downers," but they are able to focus on the good stuff and bounce back. University of Pennsylvania Professor Marty Seligman's research makes a strong case for the importance of developing a *positive explanatory style* (PES). People who have PES as opposed to NES—a *negative explanatory style*—have developed the unique ability to reframe their setbacks and tragedies by finding the good in the bad.[2]

In my "Increasing Your Personal Effectiveness" seminars I ask the participants to visualize someone who on the way to work has a minor fender bender. Once he gets to work, he whines all day long: "My poor car; it's all scratched up. What's the matter with these people? Who gave them a driver's license?" (I think that you catch my drift, especially if you have worked with someone like this.) Using all your mental energy to find the bad in the bad, that's a negative explanatory style—NES. And yes, there is lots of bad stuff once you focus on it. (Have you ever noticed that people who whine a lot have a lot to whine about? It's as if God is contemplating: "Whom should I give this problem to? Why don't I give it to John; he whines all the time anyway.")

What does a PES person do? It's that rare person who on her way to work has a terrible accident. She rolls her car over and totals it. Even though she barely makes it out alive, she hails a taxi and shows up for work. After telling you about the accident, she says: "I am sooo lucky. Been wanting a new car anyway." This is a PES person.

To manage yourself more effectively, practice the following *smart steps:*

- *Focus on the good stuff.* You are going to find more of what you're looking for.
- *Reframe your bad experiences.* You will perceive all experiences differently depending on how you frame them (just like a painting looks different with a different frame).
- *Find the good in the bad.* See the story above.
- *Tune into the triggers that cause you to feel bad.* Interrupt them or turn them off by substituting a different trigger that causes you to feel good.
- *Help others who are worse off than you.* Hopefully, this is what you do one way or another as a contrarian leader.

Motivate Thyself

Sarah Hughes, 2002 Winter Olympics ice-skating gold medalist, exemplifies this habit to the max. Getting yourself to do the things you don't want to do—getting up every day at 5:00 A.M. to practice since age six—and *not* doing what you really feel like doing—delaying gratification and reigning in impulsiveness—are what it takes to become a gold medalist or an excellent contrarian leader. In addition, if you saw Sarah's final performance, you know that she also mastered a third ingredient—the ability to get *into the zone* or a *flow state* where you shut out all external distractions and are single-mindedly focused on the task at hand. ("I just went out to have fun" were her words at the end of her flawless performance. The same attitude will enable you to lead effectively.) Combine these three skills, and you have the making of a champion at work and at home.

Here is how you can develop this habit faster:

- Treat success as the rule and failures as the exception.[3]

- Do what you don't feel like doing, and think twice before you do what you really feel like doing.
- Chase your passion, not your pay.[4]
- Laugh more often than you think is wise—especially at yourself.
- Remind yourself that how you feel is your choice. Don't give that choice away.

Empathize with Others

This habit, often referred to as *attunement, building rapport,* or *being sensitive,* is concerned with being able to recognize and respond appropriately to the emotions of others. It involves tuning into verbal as well as nonverbal cues to discern your team members' moods, emotions, and feelings and then modifying your approach accordingly. It is concerned with the ability to care—not make believe, but truly getting into someone else's moccasins and walking more than a mile in their shoes.

Here is how you can hone this habit:

- *Practice active listening.* You know you have mastered this art when you not only hear the words but also *hear* what is *not* being said.
- *Reality test, also known as mirroring.* Restate what you heard in your own words, capturing not only the words but also the feelings that go with the words. For example: "What I hear you saying is that you don't like me disagreeing with you because it upsets you." (This is a powerful anger management technique. *Do* practice it at home.)
- *Master the echo technique.* This is when you repeat what a team member says and add a question mark at the end of the sentence. Team member: "You are driving me nuts." You: "Driving you nuts?"
- *Ask open-ended questions to learn all you can about someone's "hot buttons."*
- Any time you interact with a team member, visualize the following words on his forehead: "*Make me feel important.*" Then act accordingly.

Develop Charisma

Social competence, *people skills,* or *charisma* is the ability to communicate and negotiate effectively, decrease conflict, and form strong personal bonds with team members. In other words, it is the ability to make the previous habits come together like a world-class orchestra so that team members accept and like you unconditionally.

Here are five *smart steps* that will enable you to develop charisma:

- Accept team members the way they are, not the way they ought to be.
- Catch team members doing things almost *right* and tell them about it.
- Discount team members' weaknesses. (We all have them; don't you?)
- Infect people with your contagious *positive* mood. (How you feel is a choice. Choose to be positive.)
- Give more of what you want. (Read these again and start practicing them right now.)

You know that you have developed charisma when team members' say: "I like myself best when I'm with you."

Be Honest

WorldCom, Tyco, Global Crossing, Anderson, and Enron—do I need to say more? Before you get too smug, however, you had better look at the face in the mirror. Study after study has shown that most people lie at one time or another.[5] We inflate our résumés, fudge our accomplishments, and exaggerate even inconsequential events. And when we lie, there is no trust, and without trust, you can't practice contrarian leadership. Call me old-fashioned; I believe that there is no excuse for lying. There is not even a good reason for exaggerating. If you do, you will have to talk from the head—checking your memory to make sure that you are consistent. And who can keep track of that when most of us have trouble remembering where we put our car keys. Only by getting in the habit of always telling the truth—especially if it is at your own expense—will you be able to talk from the heart—and that will set you free. Moreover, it will enhance your leadership skills—people follow people whom they can trust—and put you on the fast track in any endeavor. It also will enrich your personal relationships and, most important, will get you to like and respect yourself—the foundation for being an effective contrarian leader.

Kill Your Ego

Ego probably has destroyed more organizations than any other human emotion. (See the list at the beginning of the preceding paragraph.) I guess that this is so because ego, right along with greed and envy, is one of the most powerful destroyers of relationships. A look at history confirms that these emotions are responsible for more evil—think Napoleon, Stalin, and Hitler—and more corporate failures—think Enron, Arthur Andersen, and WorldCom—as well as more relationship killers than any other emotion. And yet you can get rid of your ego with just five powerful phrases expressed liberally and from the heart.

Here they are:

- *You are right about that.* Any time you get into a conflict, use this phrase and you will have *no* conflict ever again—guaranteed! (Just this one strategy is worth more than the price of this book.)
- *I've made a mistake.* This phrase helps you to get off your high horse gracefully. All human beings make mistakes—and since you, like all other human beings, are imperfect—I think you get it. Just because you are the leader does *not* mean that you are omnipotent. There is only one force like that in the universe—and no, it's not you.
- *I changed my mind.* It's been said that women have cleaner minds then men because they change them often. (Okay, enough with the stereotypes.) You are an evolving human being, one who is like red wine that gets better all the time—this means that you have to let go of your past beliefs.
- *I don't know.* Admit it, you don't know everything. It lets your team members know that you have high levels of self-esteem. Only people who are okay inside their own skin can admit that they don't know everything.

- *Let's agree to disagree.* This is the phrase to use if all else fails. It works especially well with the real important people in your organization—the contrarians.

Smile

Since I was the first to arrive at our company one morning, I answered the telephone. When the caller asked for accounting, I explained that it was before regular business hours, but that I would help if I could.

"What's your job?" the caller asked me.

"I'm the president," I replied.

There was a pause. Then he said, "I'll call back later. I need to talk to someone who knows what's going on."

SMART STEPS

Read this chapter again, it's full of smart steps. Just do it!

4

Don't Manage People

You manage things; you lead people.
—Admiral Grace Murray Hopper

MOST PEOPLE CRAVE TO BE LED but don't want to be managed. They want to come to work and do a good job. If on top of that they can be involved in a worthy cause, be part of a winning team, feel great about the person they report to, and in turn feel great about themselves, they are literally in work heaven. This book is all about leading more and managing less or, to be more precise, mastering 20 contrarian leadership strategies that will enable you to become a more effective leader. To find out what the difference is between management and contrarian leadership take a look at Exhibit 4-1.

So what is *your Weltanschauung,* or paradigm? (You know that a paradigm is a pair of dimes, don't you? Just kidding! The word *paradigm* comes from the Greek and refers to "a way of interpreting the world around you.") To get clarity on just how well you are practicing CL, complete the Contrarian Leadership Self-Assessment Instrument in Exhibit 4-2.

Hey, this is cool, but what *specific* leadership strategies will give me the best results? I'm glad you asked, because the answer has become a lot

Exhibit 4-1 *Managers versus Contrarian Leaders (CLs)*

Managers	Contrarian Leaders
Rely on the "tried and true"	Experiment with contrarian approaches
Maintain	Develop
Control	Trust
Direct	Inspire
Administer	Innovate
Strategy-driven	Philosophy-driven
Rely on position power	Empower
Structure/system focus	People focus
Cope with complexity	Embrace change
Focus on the bottom line	Focus on employee *and* customer satisfaction
Do things right	Do the right things right

Exhibit 4-2 *Contrarian Leadership Self-Assessment Instrument (CLSI)*

Instructions: Using the following scale, circle the numbers under the letters—SD, D, N, A, or SA—that correspond to your level of disagreement or agreement with each statement (SD = strongly disagree; D = disagree; N = neutral; A = agree; and SA = strongly agree). *Please ignore the numerical values* when making a decision. (For purposes of this instrument, *team members* are the people you work with or who report to you.)

	SD	D	N	A	SA
1. I consistently question everything.	1	2	3	4	5
2. I'm in the habit of giving my power away.	1	2	3	4	5
3. When I have to make a choice between taking care of myself or my team members, I put my team members first.	5	4	3	2	1
4. I make sure that my team members have fun at work.	1	2	3	4	5
5. I'm in the habit of taking the blame when things don't work out.	1	2	3	4	5
6. I use our mission, vision, and core values to "control" my team members' behavior.	1	2	3	4	5
7. I feel that it is not important how we play the game as long as we win.	5	4	3	2	1

	SD	D	N	A	SA
8. I encourage team members to break the rules.	1	2	3	4	5
9. I'm in the habit of motivating my team members by creating "desire" instead of "fear."	1	2	3	4	5
10. I consistently treat all my employees as if they are volunteers.	1	2	3	4	5
11. I'm in the habit of focusing on the bottom line.	5	4	3	2	1
12. Our detailed goals and objectives serve as our business drivers.	5	4	3	2	1
13. I trust all my employees and customers all the time.	1	2	3	4	5
14. I make it a practice to tie rewards to performance.	1	2	3	4	5
15. I believe that an increase in pay likely will lead to peak performance.	5	4	3	2	1
16. Instead of assigning projects, I prefer to ask for volunteers.	1	2	3	4	5
17. Customer satisfaction is the most important key to business success.	5	4	3	2	1
18. The best way to improve our profitability is to downsize.	5	4	3	2	1
19. More than half my time at work is used up by taking care of emergencies and urgent requirements.	5	4	3	2	1
20. I feel that in order to get ahead I have to be totally committed to my company.	5	4	3	2	1

TOTALS ___ ___ ___ ___ ___

GRAND TOTAL _____

Scoring Instructions: Total the numbers you have circled in the spaces provided, and come up with a grand total.

Contrarian Leadership Self-Assessment Instrument: What Your Score Means:

95–100. Wow! I'm impressed! It seems like you know how to practice CL. And since CLs are voracious lifelong learners, I know that you can't wait to learn more about it.

85–94. Excellent. You have a solid CL foundation on which to build.

75–84. Very good. You are on the right track and will learn lots of powerful new strategies from this book.

65–74. Good. But you can do better. However, you know that already. After all, that's why you are reading this book.

< 65. Okay. But you have not even begun to scratch the surface of your *leadership* potential. This is really exciting because you will get an incredible value from this book. So get ready, get set to learn and apply.

clearer as a result of exciting research reported by Daniel Goleman, coauthor of *Emotional Intelligence*.[1] Goleman and investigators from the consulting firm Hay/McBer studied a random sample of 3871 executives selected from 20,000 executives worldwide and found that the most effective leaders choose from six distinctive leadership styles, depending on the situation and what they want to get accomplished.

The research investigated how each of the six leadership styles correlated with the specific components of the organization's climate (or working atmosphere of an organization). The researchers found that leaders who used styles that had a positive impact on an organization's climate had dramatically better financial results. By the way, the organizational climate was responsible for a third of a leader's desired results. (The other two were economic conditions and competitive dynamics.)

Here, then, are the six leadership styles in order of their impact on an organization's climate or culture and the situations in which they will provide you with the best results:

> *Coercive*. This is a leader who demands immediate compliance—the "it's my way or the highway" style. This style has a very high probability of destroying your organizational climate and possibly even you. It may be useful in an emergency, a "turnaround" situation, or as a last resort with a problem employee. This leadership style has the most negative impact on the overall organizational climate. Avoid it at all costs.
>
> *Pacesetting*. This is a leader who sets extremely high standards for performance—someone who wants results yesterday. Even though this leader typically will role-model what's expected from others, it's still a climate killer. It is only successful when you work with extremely highly motivated and competent team members who know the leader extremely well. Others will feel overwhelmed and give up because they cannot see themselves reach the leader's unrealistic expectations. This style has virtually the same negative impact on the overall organizational climate as the coercive style. Use this style very sparingly.
>
> *Coaching*. This is a leader who is focused on "growing people." Coaching leaders are great delegators and are willing to put up with short-term failures provided they lead to learning and long-

term development. This style works best when you want to help
employees improve their performance or develop their long-term
strengths. This style has a relatively high positive impact on the
overall organizational climate that is virtually the same as the
democratic style. Use this style when employees are interested
and willing to learn and be coached.

Democratic. This is a leader who wants to achieve consensus
thorough participation. This style builds trust, respect, and
commitment and works best when you want to get employees to
"buy in," achieve consensus, or provide input. It does not work
when there are severe time constrains or if employees are
confused or uninformed. If handled correctly, this style has
virtually the same positive impact on the overall organizational
climate as the coaching style. Use this style when you have
ample time and work with employees who are knowledgeable
and informed.

Affiliative. This is a leader who is interested in creating harmony
and building emotional bonds with employees. This leader is a
relationship builder who is focused primarily on the people
issues of organizational life. This style works best when you
want to motivate employees, especially when they face stressful
situations or when you want to build team harmony, improve
communication, increase morale, or repair broken trust. This
style has a slightly more positive impact on the overall
organizational climate than the coaching and democratic styles.
Because this style has virtually no downside, it is the best
overall approach. Therefore, if you are in doubt, use the
affiliative style.

Authoritative. This is a leader who mobilizes people with an
incredible level of enthusiasm and a clear vision. This is a
visionary leader who gives people lots of leeway to innovate and
take calculated risks provided that they move in the direction of
the stated vision. This style works best when changes necessitate
a new vision or when employees are looking for a new
direction. This style fails when employees are more
knowledgeable or experienced than the leader or if the
authoritative style becomes overbearing. Provided that it is used

with finesse, this style has the most positive impact on the overall organizational climate. Use this style if you have a clear vision of the future and you can mobilize people to buy into your vision.

Back to our original question—Which leadership style will give you the best results? The answer, as you have just learned, is that it *depends on the situation*. However, Goleman's research has shown that leaders who have mastered four or more styles, especially the authoritative, affiliative, democratic, and coaching styles, and who can move seemlessly from one to the other depending on the situation, have the most positive organizational climates and the most effective business performance.[2] However, if you are unable to use all four styles, or if you are in doubt, use the affiliative style because it likely will keep you out of trouble and give you the results you want.

The Cost of Leadership Misalignment

Janet was brought on board as the director of sales of this small, fast-growing niche-player mail-order company. A very compassionate, warm, and friendly executive—David—who was an affiliative-type leader, led the company. David had taken over the business from his father about eight years ago and had built it from negligible sales to around $20 million in annual sales currently. He was an extremely hard worker—70-hour weeks were the norm—and his approximately 70 employees liked, admired, and even revered him. Having grown the company to its current level of success, David felt the need to bring a vice president of sales on board to help him reach the leadership team's "humongous overarching goal" (HOG) of $200 million in sales in 10 years. For the HOG to become reality, David was especially dependent on Janet, who was charged with achieving aggressive sales targets and transforming the sales department from being primarily "inbound" sales-driven—mailing out catalogs and then waiting for orders—to also becoming "outbound" focused—having a cadre of highly effective sales professionals who would establish long-term relationships with their customers and be proactive in generating sales. Janet had been a fairly obvious choice because David had gotten to know her in her role of sales manager in his sister's manufacturing business, which had been sold recently. Janet seemed to be just the right person to help the company achieve its HOG. She was very focused, very well spoken, and seemed to fit the positive organizational culture that had been built by David. After coming onboard, Janet rolled up her sleeves and went to work to reorganize the sales department. She drew up plans for outbound sales, reorganized the physical layout of the sales department, and changed the compensation system for the sales team. She also told the inbound sales manager—Tim—how she expected him to deal with employees "because what you've done in the past obviously has not worked around here." Janet also asked Tim to start monitoring the sales associates' phones. At the same time Janet focused much of her mental energy on what employees had been doing wrong and let them know about it often in an underhanded, aggressive, and public manner. It only took about three weeks before Janet and Tim had their first altercation and the first sales associate had left the company. By the end of nine months, Tim had put in his resignation—"I can't work for someone who constantly belittles me and tells me what I am doing wrong. This is getting me so upset that I have been getting sick to my stomach and even had to see a doctor who told me that I have an ulcer," said Tim. In addition to Tim, 5 of the 24 sales associates had quit as well, and complaints from others, even from customers and employees from outside the sales department, kept pouring in. It was time for David to bite the bullet and let Janet go. David concluded that Janet's coercive leadership style—which never showed up when she interacted with *him*—simply was not aligned with the organizational culture and that the human costs of keeping her—even though her ideas and the systems she had put in place seemed to be on the right track—were just too great.

Smile

Among other things, Linda was responsible for providing employees training in proper dress codes and etiquette for a midsize company. One day as she was stepping onto the elevator, another employee, rather casually dressed in jeans and a golf shirt, got on with her. Thinking of her responsibilities, Linda scolded, "Dressed a little casually today, aren't we?" The man replied, "That's one benefit of owning the company."

SMART STEPS

Vary your leadership style in accordance with the situation. During the next six months, attend a leadership course that will enable you to master the authoritative, affiliative, democratic, and coaching leadership styles. Then make it a practice to use the style that will give you the best results for a specific situation.

If in doubt, use the affiliative leadership style. If you are unable to master the authoritative, democratic, and coaching leadership styles, use the affiliative style. It has a high probability of giving you the results you want.

Check for leader-culture alignment. When hiring new managers, use situational questions and, if possible, standardized instruments to assess the leadership style of prospects. (One I like to use is the Leader Behavior Questionnaire.[3]) Then make sure that the leader's style is aligned with your organization's culture.

Use multiple interviewers whenever you hire new team members. The research is pretty clear. Your odds of selecting the best employee for the job are about 50-50 when you are the only one who is interviewing prospective employees. (You might as well flip a coin.) The reason is that we all see and hear what we want to see and hear. In addition, we tend to hire people who are most like us. (Not a good strategy—why would you need someone who is just like you?) And the only way to improve these odds is to use multiple interviewers with each interviewer asking the same questions, which are then scored and summarized to pick the top three candidates to be reinterviewed.

5

Don't Be Proud

When men are the most sure and arrogant they are commonly the most mistaken, giving views to passion without that proper deliberation and suspense which alone can secure them from the grossest absurdities.

—DAVID HUME

PRIDE—THE CHEST-THUMPING, I'm the best, we have all the answers, I'm too smart to make mistakes type of pride—is the hallmark of ineffective leaders. What I learned from Lou Holtz is this: When the team wins, the winning coach gives all his credit to the team. On the other hand, when the team loses, the coach will take the hit. One of the best ways to assess the interpersonal skills of leaders is to observe how they deal with credit and blame. Those who have their heads screwed on right realize that it's virtually impossible to get off your high horse gracefully. They also take advantage of the power of planting seeds and letting their team members nurture those seeds. And when the seeds bear fruit, highly effective contrarian leaders (CLs) make team members look like heroes, ideally in front of their peers or better yet in front of the top dog. This is, of course, one of the ways you get people to give you 111 percent. On the other hand, the interpersonal wimps hog the credit and fix the blame and can't figure out the reasons for low morale and productivity. And here's a little secret— drum roll please—listen up, I wouldn't want your competitor to hear this: If you consistently give your credit away, *you* will—over the long term— get all of it back and then some. And then you won't have to thump your chest anymore because you will be the chief executive officer (CEO).

Here is an elegant example of the cost of the pride I'm talking about in this chapter. About the time that the PT Cruiser was released, "Super-woman"—that's Marcela, my wife of over 35 years—and I were car shopping. It was time to replace Marcela's 1984 Mercedes Benz. Even though it had 180,000 miles and virtually all the original parts—including shocks, exhaust system, and so on—nothing was wrong with it. (But that's another story on "where has all the quality gone?") However, Marcela wanted something new, as well as something that would be more dependable in the snow and ice.

To get ourselves familiar with the current offerings, we stopped by the local Chrysler dealer to look at the "hot" PT Cruiser. The dealer had two on the lot, which was very exciting because the other dealers that we had visited only had pictures. The first thing that happened was that we were totally ignored while browsing on the lot. (It never fails to amaze me how little real customer service there is, especially in the automobile retail business. By the way, this is why I believe the automakers run all those obnoxious commercials. They constantly have to attract new customers because they have yet to figure out how to generate repeat customers. Since the car was locked, we walked into the showroom to get the keys. The "let's pretend we are too busy game" continued. So we walked up to the first sales desk, which was occupied by a salesman doing—you guessed it— absolutely nothing. "We'd like to look at the PT Cruiser," I said. "They are right out there," the not-so-friendly salesman said, pointing to the cars in front of the showroom. We told him that we had seen the cars but would like to test drive one or at least sit in one. "I can't let you do that," he said, puffing-up his chest in a proud, we are number one manner. Incredulous, I asked why. "They are waiting to be picked up by customers," he answered. When we said that it did not have to be those, that any PT Cruiser would do, he said, in a hey I'm doing you a big favor manner, "I don't have any. You can put your name on this list. There are about 150 people ahead of you, and when it is your turn, we'll let you know." When we explained that we were not interested in ordering a car, that all we wanted to do was sit in one and possibly test drive it, he told us that he could not help us. (Yes, you read correctly.)

Shortly after we got back from this exasperating experience, Rick Maurer, a professional colleague and author of *Beyond the Wall of Resistance*,[1] sent me an e-mail with the following words of wisdom from Lester Thurow, a professor of management and economics at the Massachusetts Institute of Technology.[2] Leaders at Nokia told Thurow the 10 reasons they dominate the cellular telephone market. Number one on the list was speed, but that's not uncommon these days. Number six was humbleness, and ten was luck. Thurow wrote: "Humbleness means that no matter how good you are, you recognize that you have a long way to go before you're really good and that you recognize that no matter how good you are, a lot of your success is traceable to good luck. Arrogance—'We make no mistakes' and 'We're on top because we are good'—is the opposite of humbleness and always leads to disaster. And in the late 1980s, no one was more arrogant about their quality control than the Japanese."

Thurow cited the Bridgestone-Firestone tragedy, Mitsubishi's covering up automobile defects for years, and the milk company, Snow Brand, poisoning people by recycling returned milk, as examples. Thurow said: "Arrogance does not just make you sloppy. It also means when you find a mistake you can't admit it."

When was the last time you saw humbleness or luck listed as major reasons why a company was successful? Thurow believes that humbleness is the most important of Nokia's core values because it is the antidote to the sin of arrogance and pride.

Humbleness obviously has not been taught to Chrysler distributors, at least not the ones we dealt with. They had a "hot car" that at the time, primarily because of its newness, had *temporary* high demand. Today it takes deep discounts to get people to buy the same cars. The temporary high demand led the sales team at the dealership we visited to be very proud or even arrogant—so proud that they were more interested in puffing out their chests rather than finding out what other cars we might be interested in looking at and test driving. (One estimate of the sales potential of every car customer is—are you ready for this—$332,000 over the life of that customer.) Now whether the lack of humbleness of this one dealership's sales team has anything to do with the poor performance of Daimler-Chrysler's stock, I certainly don't know nor claim. However, lets put it this way: Marcela and I walked out of the Chrysler showroom less than happy with a commitment that we would never buy a Chrysler no matter how good their cars. With it we took $332,000 of potential sales next door to the Toyota dealer, where we were almost treated like "customers." (Wow! What a shock!) And since research tells us that people have a habit of spreading bad customer service stories to an average of 11 other people—obviously I'm much more prolific—you don't have to be a mathematician to figure out the negative impact on that Chrysler dealer's bottom line.

Now, before you get too comfortable claiming righteous indignation, let's talk about *you*, your sales team, and your employees, especially if you are prospering in this highly competitive global economy. Are you really proud of that performance? So proud that at times your and your team members' behavior borders on arrogance? Or do all of you consume ample portions of "humble pie" on an ongoing basis? And is that reflected in the way your customers (this includes your employees) are being treated? If not, you will prove Thurow correct because "arrogance . . . *always leads to disaster.*"

Smile

If you have lots of power or money, you are probably not nearly as funny, smart, or good looking as people tell you.

SMART STEPS

Provide lots of opportunities for your team members to experiment. If they do things the "way we've always done them," your team will go into a self-destruct mode. And one of the best ways to do this is to publicly reward calculated risk taking and even making mistakes. [No, I have not lost it. One of my clients proudly gives out the coveted GUP (goof up) award.] Remember: *Whatever you reward is what you are going to get more of.*

Publicly admit to your team members when you have made a mistake. Then share what you have learned from the mistake and what specifically you will do differently *the next time.*

Banish the "we are the best" syndrome from your organization. Instead, share with your team that "All of us are like red wine; we get better all the time."

Get in the habit of telling stories which demonstrate that you believe that success is a journey, not a destination.

Get rid of the "not invented here" (NIH) concept from your team members' vocabulary. Set up an ongoing "learn from the competition" program by having your employees mystery-shop the competition. When they come back, have them report on what the competition is doing *right* that would enable you to improve your productivity and performance.

Take a look at your products and services, and put a plan into place that will begin to either revitalize or, if not possible, cannibalize your most successful ones now.

Don't Be Tough

To be humble to superiors is a duty. To equals, it is courtesy. To subordinates, it is nobility.

—BENJAMIN FRANKLIN

MANAGING PEOPLE IS A TOUGH BUSINESS that requires a tough manager. And it is true that sometimes managers have to make tough calls. Jack Welch, former CEO of General Electric (GE)—regarded by many as the most successful executive of all time—says that GE made a leap forward when it made the tough call of removing what he calls type IV leaders— "the manager who doesn't share [GE's] values, but delivers the numbers; the 'go-to' manager, the hammer, who delivers the bacon but does it on the backs of people, often 'kissing up and kicking down' during the process." These managers, according to Mr. Welch, are "the toughest to part with because organizations always want to deliver—it's in the blood—and to let someone go who gets the job done is yet another unnatural act."[1] So make sure that you do not conduct yourself as a type IV leader.

From my experience, toughness is often confused with arrogance and its partner-in-crime, ego. Both will lead to disaster. Here is a story that will demonstrate what I mean (names have been changed to protect the guilty):

The Smart Widget Manufacturing Company (SWMC), like so many others, had fallen on hard times after 9/11. Albert, the manager of one division—TSGB—had been given the order by senior management to cut 50 of his approximately 250 employees. To break the news officially to his team members, Albert called an all-hands meeting. Here is what he said:

The reason for the meeting today is a "wake-up call." Due to our poor profitability, we were asked to reduce our workforce by 50 people. The board directed today's action. The major reasons were profitability and to be a competitor in the market. SWMC's profitability is 21 percent; our competitors are 40 percent and up. We must execute.

What does a wake-up call mean? Your dreams stop. Some dreams are dreams. Some dreams are nightmares. We must wake up from the dreams. Our goal is to retool. This must be executed. The second part of the wake-up call is that we are needed, but we have to work for it. Fifty people is a deep cut. Now we must do more with fewer people. You need to be driving the goal. Don't wait for someone to tap you on the shoulder like today. You need to be in the driver's seat. This means you have to drive, but tell me if you are missing the hand brake. You also need a driver's license. Your decisions and contributions drive us. The responsibility for the future is your responsibility as well as mine. I told the managers at a retreat to manage with the right tools and drive. [In the face of this dramatic reduction, the management team had recently gone to a two-day retreat at a major resort.] Everybody must be aligned and execute. You need to have the passion to drive our future.

I am not saying that we will not cut again. This I will not promise.

To summarize: We had serious cuts. This was not easy for the management team. We tried to be fair. Tomorrow we need you, your drive, your passion, and your desire to win. We have to beat our competitors doing the best in our job.

Thank you for the wake-up call. Now we must get rid of the dreams.

After this meeting, the employees basically went into shock. Instead of productivity increasing, it decreased. Morale went into the tank. In response, I was hired to coach Albert to improve his interpersonal skills and help him to rebuild the team.

When I asked Albert the reason for the approach he used during the all-hands meeting, he told me that he wanted to let them know how bad things had gotten. "And the only way I was going to be able to communicate that was to be tough." Hence his repeated comments about the wake-up call. He simply could not understand why the employees took it so personal. "I was just trying to light a fire under them" were Albert's words.

Subsequent to this meeting, I started to coach Albert, and we began the repair process with his team members by calling another all-hands meeting. To get him ready for this meeting, I convinced Albert that there was no need to "light a fire" under his employees, nor to give them a wake-up call. "Albert," I said, "your team is hurting. They need a soft manager, someone who is caring and nurturing." Since I had found out that Albert's older son had taken ill, I advised Albert to assume that the employees in front of him were just like his sick son and that he was to speak to them from his heart, in a caring and nurturing way, as he had spoken to his ailing son earlier that day. I also encouraged him to make himself vulnerable by talking about the challenges that he was facing and to use most of his available time to focus on the needs of his employees, not on himself or the management team. Surprisingly, Albert did an extremely effective job to the point that the human resources representative told me that "she had never seen that side of Albert before." Unfortunately, the president of SWMC had already put pressure on Albert's boss to replace him. Enough pressure that even though Albert's boss generally was satisfied with Albert's performance, Albert had been replaced in less than six months from the time he made the tough comments to his team.

Even though this situation clearly called for a soft approach, I agree with management consultant William Peace, who maintains that it is hard work to be a soft manager.[2] Peace maintains that in addition to the qualities of intelligence, energy, confidence, and responsibility, managers also should be candid, sensitive, and be willing to suffer the painful consequences of unpopular decisions. Peace concluded: "Being vulnerable to the give-and-take of ordinary emotional cross-fire and intellectual disagreement makes us more human, credible, and open to change."[3] And to me the best way to function as an effective "soft contrarian leader" is to master the art and skill of persuading people to do your thing *their* way. And the best way to do that is for you to relentlessly apply the following five laws. I call them laws because, according to Robert Cialdini, author of *Influence: Science and Practice*,[4] they are based on deeply rooted human drives that have been substantiated in over five decades of scientific investigations. And most important—based on my own consulting and coaching experiences—they work.

The Law of Liking

This law maintains that *people are more likely to like people who like them*. The reason: People who are liked generate affection and good feelings, and people who feel good about themselves are more likely to comply with your wishes. The epitome of the law of liking is my daughter Nicole, who has this innate charisma, personal magnetism, or whatever you want to call it that gets people to like her—even fall in love with her—after just a short time. As a result, Nicole has the largest, most powerful network of any person I have ever met. And members of that network are always eager to help her in any way they can. You can achieve the same result by mastering three powerful strategies that will cause people to like you.

> *Strategy 1: Send out liking signals.* One of the most powerful is to smile. A smile bridges the language gap and communicates to the other party, no matter where they are from or if they even speak your language: "I'm okay, and you're okay."
>
> *Strategy 2: Become an active listener so that you can find something to like about the other person.* The reality is that all people are a composite of strengths and weaknesses, and it really does not take any more energy to find the good in people than to find the bad. To make this work, use your mental energy to focus on the good stuff in the other person, and then let her know what you found.
>
> *Strategy 3: Find what you have in common with another person and let him know about it.* Similarities establish a positive bond with others and create goodwill and trustworthiness. For example, research into the buying behavior of people has

repeatedly verified that we are more likely to buy from someone we like *and* have something in common with. And even though you may not be making your living from sales, you do sell all the time. You sell your boss on a promotion, your sell your team members on implementing a new system, and you sell your spouse on where to go for dinner.

The Law of Reciprocity

This law maintains that *whatever you give is what you're going to get.* It seems so simple yet so powerful. If you want more of something—be it performance, trust, or even love—you have to give it before you get it. Charities figured this out a long time ago. They found that by including a little gift with their solicitation letter—such as personalized address labels—they could almost double the response rates. What works for charities also will work for you. For example, if you want your team members to trust, respect, and cooperate with you, model the behavior you want, and you will get more of it. And here's a big value-add: It works in your personal life, too. For example, I have found that the way for me to get more trust, love, and joy is to give them first. The result: I've enjoyed an exceptionally positive marriage to my "Super-woman" for over 35 years.

The Law of Commitment

People are more likely to do what they commit to, especially if the commitment is in writing. I use this law in my executive coaching sessions. Recently, one of my clients was struggling with a highly valued manager—let's call him Jim—who had poor interpersonal skills that interfered with his ability to manage people. I sat down with Jim and his boss, Judy, and used a powerful technique that enabled both parties to talk frankly about their concerns. During this meeting, Jim voluntarily committed to take specific actions that would address the most critical issues raised by Judy. These commitments were written down and signed by both parties and led Jim to take actions that began to improve his ability to get along with Judy.

The second key to make this law work is to make the commitment public. Here is an exercise I learned originally from Max Bazerman, author of

Judgment in Managerial Decision Making,[5] that demonstrates this to the extreme:

Imagine yourself in a room with me and about 25 other people. I hold up a $20 bill and say: "I am going to auction off this $20 bill. Please note that this is a real $20 bill and a real auction. Bids must be made in multiples of $1 until the bidding stops, at which point the person with the highest bid must pay me the amount bid to receive the $20 bill. The only two features that distinguish this auction from others are (1) at least two people must bid, and (2) in addition to the highest bidder, the *second* highest bidder also must pay the amount he or she bid. For example, let's say that the bidding stops when Tony bid $8 and Karen bid $7. At that point Tony pays me $8 and gets the $20 bill (that means Tony made $12), and Karen pays me $7 and gets nothing (that means Karen lost $7)."

Would you make a bid? How high would you bid? I have run this auction in several programs and find that the bidding starts out with several people participating at a very aggressive pace. Once the bidding gets to about $12 to $16, most people drop out except two. And these two get into a furious competition, which incredulously almost always exceeds $20. At that point everyone is very amused except the two people who are bidding. One auction I conducted in a graduate class at the University of Maryland ended when the bid reached $51. Glad you asked. No, I don't keep the money. I use it as a prize at the end of the session.

The Law of Expertise

The essence of this law is this: *People are more likely to heed the advice of experts.* People who are perceived as experts have a greater ability to persuade others. According to a study reported by Robert Cialdini,[6] most hospital stroke patients tended to abandon the exercise routines prescribed by their physical therapists. Interviews revealed that patients were familiar with the credentials of their physicians—whose instructions they tended to comply with—but they knew very little about the qualifications of their physical therapists. The remedy: Display the academic diplomas and certificates of the physical therapists in the exercise room. The result: Exercise compliance increased by 34 percent.

You can take advantage of this law by making your expertise more visible and by sharing your prior experience and expertise with your team members and customers. However, do it in such a way that it is not perceived as bragging. A good way to do this is in social settings.

The Law of Scarcity

It is true that *people want more of what they can't have.* Any time you see "limited time," "one-of-a kind," or "act now" offers, you are face to face with the law of scarcity. Study after study has demonstrated that that which is less available is perceived as more valuable. My "Superwoman" experienced this law during our courtship when I attempted to get her interested in me. Nothing seemed to work until I showed up at a dance with another woman. All of a sudden Marcela become very interested in me.

You can take advantage of this law by letting your employees know that only the top five achievers will be selected to be on a certain team or that only those who demonstrate a certain level of performance during the next six months will receive a bonus.

Use these five laws in tandem and you will quintuple your ability to persuade and influence people and won't find a need to be a tough manager ever again.

Smile

Scott, a real pessimist, wanted to become an optimist. His friend Dennis, who was an avid skydiver, suggested that Scott learn to skydive. "There simply is nothing more optimistic than skydiving," said Dennis.

So after taking the requisite lessons, Scott was ready to make his first jump. Just before taking him up for the big day, the instructor reviewed what Scott could expect:

1. "Once we reach the proper altitude, I will give you the command, at which time you will jump."
2. "Once you are airborne, pull this cord."
3. "In the unlikely event that your chute does not open, pull the emergency cord."
4. "After you land, one of my guys will arrive in a pickup truck and take you back to your car."

They take off into the wild blue yonder, and on command, Scott jumps. Once airborne, he pulls the cord to open his parachute.

Unfortunately, the chute does not open, and Scott says to himself, "Don't panic; you were taught what to do."

So he pulls his emergency cord, and still nothing happens. At this point Scott says to himself, "This is just great. And I bet the truck won't be there either."

SMART STEPS

Develop what Professor Marty Seligman of the University of Pennsylvania calls "learned optimism" by developing your "positive explanatory style (PES)."[7] A great way to develop PES is to start each day with an attitude of gratitude. Here's how:

Start softly. Use a clock radio that plays music that is soft and pleasant to wake you up. *Don't* use a loud alarm clock. (Why would you want to start your day alarmed?)

Start slowly. Allow yourself enough time to prepare for the day's activities at a civilized pace. Get up 15 minutes before you really have to get up. That way your day will evolve in a relaxed fashion.

Focus on the good stuff. Think of three specific things you can be grateful for while sitting on the "throne." Do this every day. *Don't* worry about how original you are.

Start positively. Think about the positive things you expect to accomplish that day. *Don't* listen to news of the world's problems or worry about your own problems while you are getting your day started.

Make yourself laugh. If you read the paper while eating breakfast, skip the negative "stinking thinking" news. Skim the headlines to keep yourself informed. Read the comics before you put the paper away, and be sure to make yourself laugh. Yes, I said *make* yourself laugh.

Give love. Find something positive to say to your spouse and children, and be sure to tell them how much you love them before they or you leave home. *Don't* pick on them as the last thing before you depart. Continue the process of giving love when you get to work. (No, that is not a typo. To me effective contrarian leadership is an act of love.)

Master the PIN technique. It's a three-step mental process to help you find the good in the bad. First, when "stuff" happens or people act "weird," focus on what is positive *(P)*, then on what is interesting or innovative *(I)*, and last on what is negative *(N)*.

Give more of what you want. This is a shortcut to leadership success because life is like a mirror—whatever you put in comes right back to you. Help your team members find satisfaction in what they do, and you will be more satisfied. Love team members the way they are, and you will experience more love. You catch my drift?

Ask team members to make specific commitments and to sign their commitments, and you will get greater compliance.

Be specific and confident when you share with customers how your team has successfully helped other customers with similar problems.

Don't Play to Win

Leadership is getting someone to do what they don't want to do in order to achieve what they want to achieve.

—Tom Landry

GIVEN THE ENRON, ARTHUR ANDERSEN, WORLDCOM, and "the list goes on and on" mess, I feel a need to talk about the obvious because, apparently, it ain't very obvious. Playing to win at any price is bad business over the long term, especially since many companies are creating an unethical culture. For example, 44 percent of all nonmanagement employees who observe ethical misconduct at work, such as abusive or intimidating behavior toward employees or lying to employees, customers, vendors, or the public, do not report that misconduct because they believe that no corrective action will be taken or they fear that their report would not be kept confidential. In addition, fewer than three in five employees who did report misconduct said that they were satisfied with the organization's response. The 2003 survey of 1500 employees conducted by the not-for-profit Ethics Resource Center in Washington, D.C., further reported that although there has been the first overall drop in misconduct seen in a decade, American workers feel increased pressure—more than twice as great—to compromise ethical standards at times of mergers, acquisitions, and restructurings. The center also reported that workers and managers under the age of 30 are far less likely to report misconduct, with only 43 percent reporting such conduct compared with 69 percent for all employees. Similarly, 21 percent of younger managers with low tenure are about twice as likely to compromise ethical standards than their older counterparts.[1]

Five Habits of Highly *Unsuccessful* Leaders

Leaders who only know how to play to win often lose—because they begin to see themselves as omnipotent, able to control their own and their companies' destiny. Not sure what I'm talking about? Think about perfectly good companies that were run into the ground, such as Enron, Arthur Andersen, WorldCom, Tyco, and Rubbermaid. They were all run by perfectly intelligent and competent CEOs who wanted to win and instead lost billions of dollars of other people's money. Their desire to win came about because they all practiced the following five specific habits of highly *unsuccessful* leaders.[2]

1. They Cultivate an Unethical Culture

Hey, wipe that yawn off your face. This clearly is not obvious. Look at all the giant corporations that flamed out in the early 2000s. There is no getting away from it, whatever you—the leader—do will be emulated by your team members. And just a few bad apples can very quickly bring your company, organization, or department to its knees, especially if it is one that sustains itself on intellectual capital, like most companies do today. (In other words, when a factory is run into the ground, you still have a factory; when an Internet or service company goes kaput, it is gone—think of all the dot-coms that went down the drain.)

Of course, if you ask people if they are ethical, everyone will raise their hands. (See for yourself. Ask this question at your next all-hands meeting.) On the other hand, see who will vote in the affirmative to this question: "You are pulling out of a parking space and ever so slightly touch the car next to you. You get out and notice that it actually produced a pretty long scratch. You look around and are convinced that no one noticed. How many of you will put a note on the other car giving your name, address, and telephone and insurance numbers before you drive off?" (To keep responses anonymous, ask participants to write their answer on a three by five card and pass it to you.) The few, if any, positive responses will startle you. You see—being ethical is nonnegotiable if you are a contrarian leader (CL). You can't just act ethically if someone is around or if it is convenient or expedient—because, as I learned in the speaking business, the microphone is always on. Let me explain.

I was conducting a full-day seminar for an audience of about 100 people—if memory serves me right—in Minot, North Dakota, and at about midmorning the participants were working on an interactive exercise. I used that time to go to the bathroom so that I could be available for audience members during their break times. This time, however, was different because I had forgotten to turn off my lavaliere wireless microphone. Of course, as luck would have it, there was another gentleman in the bathroom at the same time. So we had a lively discussion while standing at the urinal, until someone from the audience came in to let me know that my mike was still on. When I returned, red-faced and embarrassed, virtually the entire audience was rolling in the aisles. (Well maybe not quite, but they did have a heck of a good laugh at my expense.)

The same applies to your behavior—your ethics are always showing, and your team members are always—yes I mean always—taking their cue from you, even if you don't think they are watching. And if you don't like that, get out of leadership now! You'll never be great at it because great leaders will do the right thing, even if it is at their expense.

2. They Think That They Are "Hot Stuff"

Unsuccessful leaders think that they or their services or products are the hottest thing since sliced bread and that their customers or team members can't do without them. They forget that any success always has a component of luck—being in the right place at the right time. They forget that they—just like all other human beings—tend to externalize failure and internalize success.

A high-tech global company I've been working with comes to mind. Until the reality of the marketplace began crashing in, the leaders of this company thought that their employees were lucky to have the privilege to work for them—"Hey, we do neat stuff, and you can't work for anyone else that lets you play with cutting-edge technologies the way we do." The leaders' feelings about the company's customers were pretty much the same—"You are lucky to have the opportunity to use our products, so be grateful and stop complaining about some of the glitches in our applications."

These leaders are so full of themselves that they avoid eating a slice of humble pie at all costs and instead begin to believe their own media packets. The fact is—here comes what you don't want to hear—being an effective leader takes persistence and hard work and has nothing to do with being hot stuff.

3. They Act Like Monkeys

These leaders see no evil, hear no evil, and speak no evil. Jim Collins, author of *Good to Great* and *Built to Last*,[3] has spent years figuring out what causes companies to succeed over the long run. And according to him, the key sign that distinguishes great companies from mediocre ones is how the leaders deal with reality. Are they dealing with the brutal facts or acting like monkeys attributing the facts to something or someone else. An example of how to do it right is Andy Grove of Intel. When the Japanese were taking their memory chip business away from Intel in the late 1980s, Grove faced the brutal facts and decided to abandon Intel's cash cow and instead switch to the manufacture of microprocessors.

An example of how to do it wrong in the extreme is NASA. According to the final report by the *Columbia* Accident Investigation Board, Linda Ham, the head of the mission management team, told her colleagues that she saw no need to obtain a better image of the damage done to the ill-fated *Columbia* spacecraft or to attempt to rescue the astronauts because "I don't think there is much we can do."[4] This comment resulted in everyone acting like monkeys and ultimately caused the death of all the astronauts and destruction of the spacecraft. Worse, they had done it all before in 1986 when the *Challenger* exploded, with apparently few lessons learned.

4. They Make Poor Decisions Because They Are Too Successful

Leaders who have found a "tried and true" method tend to stick with it even when it no longer produces optimal results for them. According to

Ram Charan and Jerry Useem, authors of *Why Companies Fail,*[5] studies show that people are less likely to make high-quality decisions after long periods of success. Enron, Lucent, WorldCom, NASA, and Polaroid are examples of this phenomenon. They all made it to the top and then attempted to continue to replicate what had worked in the past. The reason? The leaders of those organizations are just like the rest of us: They are human. And all people tend to resist surrendering their mental models—their *Weltanschauung*—especially those that have provided them with dramatic positive results in the past. A textbook example is Bernie Ebbers of WorldCom. He had found a "tried and true" method for growing his company primarily through acquisitions. And he continued to do that— instead of managing what he had acquired—at such a frantic pace—75 acquisitions in all—that it finally began to unravel, and the rest, as they say, is history.

5. They Build a "It's My Way or It's the Highway" Organizational Culture

Highly unsuccessful leaders squash dissent at any price. And team members who do not want to buy in are shown the door. As a result, employees fear the boss more than the competition and refuse to tell the truth with dire consequences. In this rapidly changing, highly competitive global marketplace, dissent is good—no wait, it's absolutely essential. No one person, even the boss, has all the answers. If you need proof of this, think of Enron.

Smile

Phrases used by highly unethical interviewees:

> *Phrase:* I take pride in my work.
> *Meaning:* I blame others for my mistakes.
> *Phrase:* I am very adaptable.
> *Meaning:* I've changed jobs a lot.
> *Phrase:* I'm highly motivated to succeed.
> *Meaning:* The minute I find a better job, I'm outta here.

SMART STEPS

Any time you are confronted with any ethical decision—the ones that are in the "gray zone"—ask yourself this question: How would you feel if this decision were headlined tomorrow morning in the *Wall Street Journal?* If the answer is "I would feel great about it," go do it. If the answer is "I would feel terrible about it," don't do it. And if the answer is "I'm not sure how I would feel about it," then ask yourself the following four questions:

1. Is the decision I'm about to make in accordance with my company's mission, vision, and core values—our organizational philosophy?

2. Is the decision I'm about to make good for the customer?

3. Is the decision I'm about to make good for the organization?

4. Is the decision I'm about to make good for me?

If all four answers are "Yes," go do it. If any answer is "No" or "Not sure," ask your mentor, coach, board of advisors, or board of directors. If it is the latter, make sure that the board is truly independent. For starters, this means that it typically meets without you.

Get yourself a coach or mentor—anyone whom you have given permission to tell you what you *don't* want to hear. (The people I coach have to put this in writing.) Then listen to your coach carefully and take action.

Turn employees into company watchdogs. Have someone from outside your company conduct an employee survey at least once a year. Then act on the findings.

To avoid disaster and improve the quality of your decisions, *appoint a rotating devil's advocate (DA) in all decision-making meetings.* It's the DA's job to argue a contrary point of view, especially to any of *your* proposed decisions.

Publicly admit to mistakes you have made. It gives your team members permission to go public with their mistakes.

Celebrate—not squash—whistle-blowers.

Aggressively hire minorities and celebrate diversity of opinion.

Make working more than 50 hours a week the exception, not the rule, and publicly celebrate employees who demonstrate work-life balance. For example, celebrate individuals who take their vacations, achieve high levels of performance without working overtime, and those who have achieved milestone wedding anniversaries. (Remember to role model these actions.)

Ask yourself: "If I got fired, what would my replacement do?" Then get busy doing that now.

Practice open-book management.[6] Your employees have to know what's going on if you want them to help make things better.

Don't Prove Yourself

I believe that the first test of a truly great man is his humility. I don't mean by humility, doubt of his power. But really great men have a curious feeling that the greatness is not of them, but through them. And they see something divine in every other man and are endlessly, foolishly, incredibly merciful.

—John Ruskin

CHARLES HAD FINALLY LANDED HIS NEW JOB. (Even if you haven't just landed a new job, read this anyway because there is lots of good advice that you'll be able to apply in your current job.) It may not have been his dream job, but it came close. After all, he had worked hard for years to become the vice president of operations. Finally, he made it and in a highly respected midsize company that was a leader in its field. Needless to say, he felt great, and he couldn't wait to prove to the president that he made the right decision to bring him on board. After all, during the what seemed like forever interview process, the president—Butch Malone—had emphasized over and over again that Charles was being hired to produce results. Butch had emphasized to Charles that his go-go company was in dire need of an infusion of energy, talent, and aggressive production quotas. And Charles just knew that he was the ideal person to deliver the goods. After all, Charles was able to achieve dramatic improvements in performance and profitability for his previous employer, so he knew that he could do it again.

Charles rolled up his sleeves to demonstrate his singular passion for improving the bottom line and to prove to Butch that his predecessor—Jamie—obviously was the wrong person for the job. In fact, Charles planned to tell his management team that results must be improved and that he wouldn't tolerate the laid-back attitude that seemed to prevail under Jamie's leadership. To let them know that he meant business, Charles also planned to ask each one of his direct reports to have an aggressive productivity improvement plan on his desk within two weeks and to advise his management team that he planned to address all employees within two weeks to let them know that he wouldn't tolerate anything less than 111 percent performance as long as he was in charge.

Sounds familiar? If not, perhaps take another look in the mirror, because this scenario has played over and over again in companies with which I have consulted. And all I can say is: Not so fast hotshot. Even though Charles was asked to achieve dramatic improvements in performance, his approach likely will backfire and give him just the opposite results. Instead of using Charles's approach, you can have a dramatic impact on an organization and achieve your goals if you forget about proving anything to anyone and instead use the following 11 steps during your first 30 to 60 days in any new leadership position.

Step 1: Walk Softly and Carry No Stick

There's gold in them thar hills. And you will find the gold by becoming a voracious learner and active listener during your first 30 days. And by the way, this is a once-in-a-job opportunity that you will never be able to replicate as long as you are with this company. The reason is what psychologist call *scotomas*—"blind spots." After you've been with an organization for a while, you will never see these things again. To find the gold, walk around with a notebook and record everything that strikes you as ineffective, wasteful, redundant, quirky, unproductive, and so on. Now here comes the important stuff: No matter how ineffective you perceive anything to be, don't change anything just yet, and *keep your mouth shut!*

Step 2: Talk Less, Listen More

Meet with all team members on an individual basis. Prior to the meetings, prepare an informal survey that will enable you to ask consistent questions, and record the answers to such questions as: What are your goals and aspirations? What stands in your way of doing a great job? What do you like about this company? What do we do really well? What could we do better? What drives you nuts around here? What do you feel could be done to improve results? What is one thing you would change if you had my job? Conclude each meeting by telling each team member how much you value her and how you would like to be able to count on her to help you get started on a positive note. Avoid, at this point, outlining your goals. Let the initial meetings focus on them, not you.

Step 3: Look for Themes

Analyze the data you collect. Look for themes. What are the issues and concerns that are raised over and over again? Identify the top three concerns, and start asking how they can best be addressed in your subsequent discussions and meetings with your team members.

Step 4: Do the Work

Schedule yourself to work every major function in your organization. For example, if you have a warehouse, spend a full day with the warehouse employees, and work every major station from receiving to packing to shipping. (No groaning please. How are you going to understand what your frontline team members have to put up with if you have not walked in their shoes? No, having done it once 15 years ago does not count.)

Step 5: Catch Your Predecessor Doing Things *Right*

While recording all the bad stuff, also find what's been done *right* so that you can extend praise for a job well done to all those who deserve it. Especially go out of your way to publicly acknowledge what your predecessor did *right*. At all costs, avoid criticizing anyone or anything during the first 30 days. Let me say this again, because if you miss this one, you will handicap yourself for a long time to come: *Do not say anything bad about anyone or anything during the first 30 days!* You simply don't know the organization well enough, nor do you understand the real reasons why things are done the way they are. So say something positive or say nothing at all. (This advice will serve you well anytime, anyplace.)

Step 6: Get to Know the Organizational Culture

Lots of things go on in organizations because of the culture or climate. (Culture is what employees do when the boss is not around.) Behavior patterns in organizations are created by what leaders reward, ignore, or punish. ("What you reward is what you get" is an axiom that you can take to the bank.) The only problem, as I find out over and over again in my consulting work, is that managers frequently reward behavior they *don't* want. For example, they lament that people won't pull together as a team. When you take a closer look, you find that what gets rewarded is individual performance. As a result, you get—glad you're catching on.

Step 7: Trial Balloon Your Vision for the Future

Reflect on how your vision for your organization will "fly" in light of what you have learned in steps 1 through 6. Try out your vision on your organizational early adaptors—the people who love change—during one-on-one meetings. Revise accordingly. This does not mean that you have to reduce or eliminate what you plan to get accomplished. It does mean that you may have to change your execution strategy. For example, if the organization has a culture of being slow to change and being risk-adverse, you may have to work harder at getting early adaptors to buy in *before* you make your vision for the future public.

Step 8: Share Your Vision

Having completed steps 1 through 7, you are now ready to conduct your all-hands meeting. Start off by making specific individuals in the organization into heroes by telling stories of what they and your predecessor have done in the past that you value. (Your stories should align with your vision and be specific.) Share your vision, goals, and commitment for a new future. [Since less is more, ideally, have only one humongous overarching goal (HOG)—more in Chapter 12.] Publicly thank those who have bought into your vision for their support. Be sure to communicate the "what's in it for them" (WIIFM), and do it with sincerity and passion. Above all, speak in inclusive terms—we *not* I. In this way, you avoid "I disease." (You may want to have your coach or trusted adviser count the number of "I's" you use when you speak to your team.) Open it up for questions, and involve your previously established support system in answering questions. Since the real questions won't be asked until they trust you, get the process going with three by five cards on which team members write their questions anonymously. Then shuffle the cards and read and answer as many questions as time allows. Be sure to be candid, concise, and considerate. Listen carefully to what is *not* being said. Conclude the meeting by asking for their help and support.

Step 9: Walk Your Talk

Make sure that you breathe, act, and live your vision and demonstrate your commitment to the HOG at every opportunity. People will pay more attention—no wait, they will pay *much* more attention—to what you do than to what you say. And if there is a disconnect between what you say and what you do, they will ignore what you say, doubt your integrity, and become cynical. And you will give them an excuse not to support you or even to work against you.

Step 10: Celebrate More Than You Think Is Wise

Publicly celebrate those who move the organization closer to the attainment of *their* vision and strategic goal. (Note the emphasis—at this point your team members must feel that it is their vision and goal.) Reinforce it all with stories of individuals and teams who have made a difference. And celebrate at every opportunity.

Step 11: Go for the Long Term

Stay positive even in the face of temporary setbacks. (They surely will come.) Keep focusing on the progress that has been made over the long term. Don't let the naysayers dissuade you from your course. Every organization has them.

As long as you have the support of about 75 percent of your management team and about two-thirds of your team members, you likely will achieve the dramatic improvements in performance and profitability for which you were hired. And you will have done it without trying to prove yourself.

Smile

Steve had just been hired as the new president of a midsized high-tech company. The president who was stepping down met with Steve over lunch and presented him with three numbered envelopes. "Open these in the numbered order if you run into a problem you don't think you can solve," advised the outgoing president.

Initially, things went along pretty smoothly, but six months later, sales started to tank, and Steve was getting desperate. Then he remembered the envelopes. He opened the first envelope, and it read, "Blame your predecessor."

So Steve called a press conference and tactfully blamed the previous president. Satisfied with his comments, the press and Wall Street responded positively, sales began to pick up, and the problem was soon behind him.

About a year later the company was again experiencing serious product problems. Having learned from his previous experience, Steve opened the second envelope. The message read, "Reorganize," which he did. And the company, with the help of Wall Street, turned around again.

After several consecutive profitable quarters, the company once again fell on difficult times. Steve went to his office, closed the door, and opened the third envelope, which said, "Prepare three envelopes."

SMART STEPS

Hey, take another look. This chapter actually has 11 very specific and powerful *smart steps*. What are you waiting for?

Practice KID, not KITA

Leaders often forget that people arrive on the scene predisposed to do a good job.

—Lionel Tiger

When you get down and dirty—and who doesn't want to do that—there are only two ways to manage people: a kick in the ass (KITA), or fear, and a kick in desire (KID). Fear causes employees to move away from something—which does not work. (Quick, *don't* think of a green dinosaur! What did you think of? I bet you thought of a green dinosaur. I know, I've tried it with thousands of audience members.) Moreover, the plain old truth is that you can't get away with using fear anymore, not even in the military. Just this morning a headline on the front page of the *Washington Post* read: "Embattled Naval Academy Chief Resigns." The reason: Vice Admiral Richard Naughton "had embarrassed and humiliated subordinates with his leadership style."[1] (Having served in the U.S. Army Medical Department and retired as a Lieutenant Colonel, that is a real wow to me!) Now stop and think for a moment, if a vice admiral in the Navy can't get away with KITA, what makes you think you can? The other way to lead people—KID—gets people to move *toward* something. And this works.

I like to ask participants: How many of you believe that fear works? It's amazing that about 30 to 45 percent of the hands go up. (And those are the honest ones.) When I can be a fly on the wall—that is, when I'm consulting—I find that the number of managers who use fear as a way to motivate employees is even higher. (I know we don't use physical KITAs anymore; however, there are many subtle forms of KITA, such as "No extra time off," "You'll do it because I say so," and "I decide who attends conventions in the desirable and undesirable locations"—the list goes on.)

To have participants discover the consequences of fear, I like to do a role play. It involves a "boss"—the kind of boss who is spelled backwards "double SOB"—usually played by me, and a volunteer, let's call him Jason, who plays the role of my direct report. We set it up so that the boss—me—is visiting Jason's office. While walking through the office, I notice a wad of paper on the floor. I turn to Jason and say, "Pick that up." Jason responds, "Do I look like I'm one of the cleaning crew? That's housekeeping's job, not mine" (well, you catch my drift). At this point I turn to Jason and say emphatically—some would call it nastily—"Pick that up or you can pick up your paycheck on Monday." Of course, Jason picks it up. Next I ask Jason and the audience, "What are you going to do just as soon as I leave?" Here are some of the responses:

- "I'm going to get even with you. I'm going to throw more than just paper on the floor."
- "I'm going to say bad things about your mama."
- "I'm going to tell my team members what a jerk you are."
- "I will kick someone else's cat."
- "I'm going to polish my résumé and start looking for a new job."

The last comment is the most important because it gets to the essence of what happens when you use fear as a leadership model. And this is important, so listen up: *Your good people will leave you!* Your good people, I call them "water walkers," can go right across the street and get paid more than you are currently paying them. What about the losers? That's right, they'll stay. They can't afford to leave, because no one else will hire them. Are you seeing the light here? If you want a bunch of unmotivated, demoralized, good-for-nothing slackers, go ahead and keep using fear as a management model.

Practicing any from of KITA today surely will get you in even more trouble in this era of employee mobility, where only 42 percent of the nation's employees consider themselves loyal to their jobs and about a fourth plan to stay at their current job for only two years. Why? According to a nationwide study by the Hudson Institute and Walker Information of Indianapolis, 56 percent of 2300 employees surveyed feel that their employers fail to show concern for them—a subversive kind of KITA—only 45 percent say that their employers treat them fairly, and a mere 41 percent feel that their employers trust them. These feelings will have a debilitating impact on your performance and bottom line.[2]

The ramifications of KITA, however, can be much more serious—it can kill. In an independent study, two Princeton University professors found broad and consistent evidence that tires made at the Decatur Firestone plant during a period of serious labor unrest were more likely to fail than tires made at the same plant at any other time or at any other Firestone plant. (The labor unrest came about when Firestone management pressed employees for wage cuts *and* 12-hour shifts. Workers struck, and management brought in replacements. After more than a year, labor capitulated and returned to work at lower wages and 12-hour shifts alongside the replacements.) The result: "Tires made during the labor strife were 376 percent more likely to prompt a complaint to the National Highway Transportation Safety Administration [and] customers with tires made during the labor dispute were more than 250 percent as likely to seek compensation from Firestone for property damage or injury blamed on faulty tires than were customers of tires made there [the Decatur plant] during more peaceful times." In addition, the researchers estimated that "40 lives were lost" as a result of the faulty tires. Firestone is still paying for that KITA today.[3]

KITA Par Excellence

This incident has stuck with me for years. I was to give a motivational presentation at an end-of-year celebration event for a Fortune 500 company. The company truly had an awesome year. The entire division was invited to a full day of celebration at a local four-star hotel. After everyone had their morning coffee, they were ushered into a large ballroom that had been converted into a make-believe football stadium. The band was playing, cheerleaders were cheering, popcorn was popping, and all the executives were dressed in sports uniforms. The energy was incredibly high. People were jumping and clapping as they recognized the teams and individuals who had accomplished extraordinary results during the preceding year. Corporate leaders exhorted the troops, and everyone was supercharged.

Then the attendees were served a first-class lunch, followed by two internationally recognized motivational speakers, who electrified what was already a highly energized crowd. Everyone was feeling great about themselves, great about the company, and great about the future. Then they bid farewell to the retiring division president with a traditional ceremony as a vice president from the home office lauded him for his many great accomplishments. During the closing comments, the vice president announced that he was taking over the division. His next words were: "We will be reorganizing, so we can become lean and mean and stay competitive. I expect that we will reduce this division by about 40 percent during the next several months. That means we'll have a lot to do, and I need to be able to count on each and every one of you to give me 100 percent. Does any one have any questions?"

As may be expected, there were no questions. Instead, the room was quiet—so quiet that you could hear a pin drop. The employees were so stunned that everyone was speechless. At that point the party was over—literally. I couldn't believe that someone in that high of a position could be so incredibly insensitive and simply not have a clue as to how and when to deliver such a devastating message appropriately. Clearly, if there was an award for "practicing KITA Par Excellence," this vice president deserved an Oscar.

What's the alternative to the KITA, or fear, model? Create desire—KID! Let's go back to our role play. I ask the audience: What if people who picked up paper from the floor could take it to a central location and get paid $5 for every deposit? Would there be any paper on the floor? Of course, you also may not have any on your desk. This is the paradox of leadership: Every action you take as a leader almost always has an unintended side effect. (Think of the devastating side effects of stock options.) Now paying someone $5 for picking up trash maybe a bit extreme, but it's a great way to illustrate the importance of getting people to *want* versus *have to* do something. Desire is a powerful motivator that gets people to take action without the boss being around.

One of my clients creates desire using a unique merit program. This system—which works equally well whether you head up a team of 12 or a company of 120,000—has enabled the company virtually to do away with the fear-based disciplinary system so common in most organizations. Exhibits 9-1 and 9-2 show what the company uses instead.

Exhibit 9-1 *Sample Merit Program*

Awards and benefits at XYZ Company will be based on our merit program. Merit is determined from the number of points you earn in five categories. Categories are weighted differently based on the importance to our company and how well they help us achieve our mission, vision, core values, and critical success factors. All employees automatically participate. Individual summary scores for each category will be announced and posted on a monthly basis. Note: *You* directly or indirectly influence each category. In other words, *how well you do is up to you!* The five categories are

1. Revenue-producing, productivity-increasing, or money-saving suggestion submitted in writing.

One suggestion, *feasible* but not implemented	50 points
One suggestion valued at $100 or more	75 points plus 5% cash bonus
One suggestion valued at $1000 or more	100 points plus 5% cash bonus
One suggestion valued at $5000 or more	125 points plus 5% cash bonus
One suggestion valued at $15,000 or more	200 points plus 5% cash bonus

2. Skill acquisition, lifelong learning, and training.

External training sessions attended	25 points/session
Company training sessions attended	50 points/session
Approved college course attended (C grade)	50 points/course

Continued

Exhibit 9-1 Continued

Approved college course attended (B grade)	100 points/course
Approved college course attended (A grade)	200 points/course
Cross-training, mastered a new *critical* skill	100 points/skill
Cross-training, mastered and working in new *critical* skill	200 points/skill

3. Delivering extraordinary service.

Reported by someone *inside* the company	50 points/report
Reported by anyone *outside* the company (customer/ vendor, etc.)	100 points/report

4. Attendance during one calendar year.

Four unscheduled absences	20 points
Three unscheduled absences	40 points
Two unscheduled absences	60 points
One unscheduled absences	80 points
No unscheduled absences	100 points

5. Giving "111 percent" (Sample submission form in Exhibit 9-2.)

   "111 percent" recognition cards may be given to you by a team member, customer, or team leader for a special service rendered in a time of need or when you have gone beyond the expected— given 111 percent. Each card is worth *10 points when you receive it* and *5 points when you give one* to a team member. Team members who accumulate more than ten 111 percent cards per month will be recognized in our monthly all-hands meeting and receive an elegant 111 percent lapel pin. Extra 111 percent pins may be traded for valuable prizes. Click on our Web site to find out the many special prizes available. Submission forms must be forwarded to Human Resources within two days from the day of receipt.

Thank you for giving us your 111 percent.
MAKE It a WINNING Year!

___

Exhibit 9-2 *111 Percent Recognition Form*

___

Please print.

TO: _____

From: _____ Employee _____

Customer/Vendor _____ Mgr. _____

Thanks for giving 111 percent! It was a big help and deserves special recognition!

On _____ you gave 111 percent by

_____

_____

Thanks again for a job exceptionally well done!

_____

(Your signature) _____ (Date) _____

___

Still can't distinguish between fear (KITA) and desire (KID)? Just think of what it takes to move a five-ton elephant. You can get behind the elephant and use your raw power—in management that's called *position power*, which you get any time someone gives you the title of manager or supervisor—to push the elephant. Are you visualizing this? Great. Because I want to ask you: Is this a good place to be? Noooooooo. I don't think so. (If you don't get it, you are not visualizing this!) Or you can reach in your pocket, take out a handful of peanuts, and get in front of the elephant. This is called *desire*. Which will be more likely to move the elephant? (This is a no-brainer, isn't it?) The "Smart Steps" that follow will enable you to create desire in your team members so that they *want* to come to work—not have to—which will make a world of difference.

Smile

Conversation between a consultant and a manager:

> *Consultant:* Do you have a plan for retaining your best team members?

Manager: I do my best to belittle them consistently until they believe that no other employer will hire them.

Consultant: Doesn't that demoralize them?

Manager: Yes, but if everyone is demoralized, no one can tell the difference.

SMART STEPS

Catch your team members doing things almost right! (I know you've heard this before—so why are you not doing it?) Get away from the mind-set that your job is to fix people. Your job is to build your team members' positive self-esteem. And nothing does this faster than having them experience the sweet taste of success. (It's like the chicken and the egg—which came first, high levels of self-esteem or peak performance?)

Measure job satisfaction at least once a year. And put a plan into effect that increases it by 10 percent every year until about 95 percent of your team members are "highly satisfied." This is important. If your company does not do this, get busy and do it for the part of the organization for which you are responsible.[4]

Provide team members with career growth opportunities either in your organization or another. I want you to send your best team members to another department of your company before they get bored and leave. And if there are no growth opportunities anywhere within your organization, take the radical step and refer them to another company. (No, that is not a typo.) Would you rather get stuck with team members who can't get a job anywhere else or those whose morale is shot because there is no career advancement? Besides, this is how you get other companies to refer more of their best people to you. (Remember the law of reciprocity? *If you want to get more of something, you've got to give it first.*)

Ask for volunteers to serve on a "Fun Team" that is responsible to ensure that what you and your team members do is fun. Because if it's fun, it gets done.

Spend at least 33 percent of your time with your team members. Another third should be spent with your customers. That leaves you 33 percent of your time to create trouble—such as writing rules and standard operating procedures (SOPs).

Show a real interest in your team members' personal lives. Do you really believe that they leave their personal problems at home? If you do, I've got a bridge to sell you. When you take a real interest in your team members, their morale will go up, your turnover will go down, and your team will become more productive. And guess what will happen to you and your bottom line?

Ask your team members often

> "What can I do to make your job easier?"

> "What stands in your way of giving 111 percent?"

> "Are we having fun yet?"

Then do what you can to remove the obstacles that stand in their way of delivering excellence. And if you can't help, tell them why.

Love, yes I said love, *your team members the way they are, not the way they ought to be.* Mastering just this one smart step will be worth the price of this book many times over.

If this is still too much to remember, let me boil it down to the platinum rule: *Always treat team members the way they would like to be treated.* When uncertain, impose two tests:

1. Would you like it if someone did this to you?

2. Would you feel proud if your actions were reported on the front page of you local newspaper?

If the answer is "No" to either question, don't do it. Period!

Don't Have People Work for You

The most powerful leadership strategy of all time: Treat all employees as if they are volunteers.

—WOLF J. RINKE

WATCH YOUR MOUTH! People don't work *for* you; they certainly don't work *under* you; and they are not your subordinates. All of us work for only one person—ourselves. The reason that you want to watch your language is that it gives people a look into your soul and lets them know what you are really all about.

However, this is a minor point. I want to take you to another level by sharing the single most important event that has enabled me to transform myself from an "it's my way or the highway" autocratic manager to becoming a contrarian leader (CL).

How I Saw the Light

Having served in the Army Medical Specialist Corps for some 12 years, I found myself coasting. The challenge was waning, I was not stretched to the max, and so I was no longer "juiced." I knew that I could retire in eight years, so I did not want to throw 12 years of service down the drain. Besides, I had a three-year commitment to pay the military back for supporting my Ph.D. So I got heavily involved in my professional organization. Within several years I was a board member and the chair for one of the divisions—the Council on Education. In that role, the board looked to me to implement new standards of education, which had been in limbo for countless years. There were 12 professionals on my committee, all highly educated, all volunteers, and all having their own agenda. I quickly became aware that all the "crutches" that I relied on as an autocratic manager did not work. For example, one of my committee members, let's call her Julie, was really gung-ho. Anytime there was a project to be done, she was the first to volunteer. There was only one minor problem—Julie seldom delivered. Forget delivering on time; she just did *not* deliver. At work, when any of my employees did that, I could counsel them, and if that didn't work, I could use the ultimate crutch—I could fire them. Trying that with Julie, however, produced just the opposite results. Her response: "Hey I don't need this. I'm outa here—more time with the family." One of my most powerful crutches was gone.

As an autocratic manager, however, I had others. I could withhold pay raises and other benefits such as going to training, getting a corner office, and so on. In any event, Andre, another committee member, had this inconsiderate habit of showing up late or not at all for our committee meetings. So I used my other big crutch. I told Andre that I was going to cut his pay. Andre's response: "Now let's see, zero from zero is still zero pay." And then it hit me—my autocratic crutches simply did not work with volunteers. I had to develop an entirely different skill set to motivate these people to get things done (see the steps below). And after I had mastered them, a really big light went on for me. This was not just a light; it was a defining moment that enabled me to transform myself from an autocratic manager into a contrarian leader. Are you ready for it? This is *big*—drum roll please!

Treat all employees as if they are volunteers.

Now stop and think, what would you say to your team members if indeed they were volunteers? How about: "Please." "Thank you!" "Can I count on you?" "I need your help." "I really appreciate what you've done." "Thanks for being on my team!" "Thanks for showing up." And now the one that blows the autocratic managers away: "Could you do me a favor?" This one just doesn't sit well with lots of managers. Here are some of the things they have said to me: "What are you talking about? You're paying them, they owe you a good job," "You've got to be nuts. They are not doing you any favor. It's their job," and so on and so on. All are really good arguments, and all are really, really incorrect. (If you agree with any of these, its time to wake up and smell the coffee because the only thing pay will do is get people to show up and stay with you. Not bad, but certainly not peak performance.) And the fastest way to achieve peak performance is to treat all employees as if they are volunteers.

How to Treat Employees Like Volunteers

Give People Something to Be Passionate About

People volunteer and devote inordinate amounts of energy, time, and resources if they are passionate about a cause they believe in. You can engage the same passion in your employees by having them align themselves with the passion of the founder—think Jeff Bezos at Amazon[1]—or the passion of the culture of the organization—think Recreational Equipment Incorporated, better known as REI[2]—or the passion driven by the corporate philosophy—think Johnson & Johnson. By the way, the latter two are preferred ways of stimulating internal motivation because sooner or later the chief executive officer (CEO) retires or departs for less positive reasons—think Martha Stewart, Bernie Ebbers of WorldCom, or Samuel Waksal of Imclone. And the way to institutionalize this is to build a positive organizational culture.

Build a Positive Organizational Culture

This is a culture where people *want* to come to work. Virtually all the successful companies I have ever consulted with accomplish this by taking employee job satisfaction very seriously. Most measure it at least once a year, several tie compensation of managers to the level of employee satisfaction, and virtually all use a wide variety of informal systems such as "breakfast with the boss," employee "town hall meetings," schmoozing with employees, functional suggestion boxes, and so on. In short, do whatever you can to keep your finger on the pulse of how satisfied your employees are. Lest you think this is frivolous, studies now show that there is a positive correlation between level of employee satisfaction and customer satisfaction. In other words, if your employees are satisfied, your customers will be satisfied, your sales with increase, and your bottom line will improve. Herb Kelleher, former CEO of Southwest Airlines, said it best: "If we ever lose our culture, we will have lost our most valuable competitive asset."[3]

Case in point: Dennis Madsen started as a part-time employee stocking shelves 36 years ago at REI. Today he is the president and CEO of the 6300-employee, $735 million cooperative that sells specialty gear to avid campers, hikers, climbers, and others with a passion for the great outdoors. This is the same company that has shown up on the Fortune 100 list of the "100 best companies to work for" six years in a row. The secret, according to an interview with Dennis Madsen in the *Harvard Business Review,* is getting the culture right. "Employees can get benefits and incentives anywhere, but it's harder for them to find a place where they can totally immerse themselves in the culture. We attract outdoors-oriented employees who sustain the culture and attract even more like-minded employees. They share the same interests and values; they're committed to the environment, to the community, to work-life balance, and to having fun outside."[4]

Take Your Mission, Vision, and Core Values Very Seriously

Companies that attract "volunteers" stand for something that employees can identify with and get passionate about. And only passionate employees will deliver consistently excellent service and improve the bottom line. This strategy is analogous to developing a brand that is identified with certain attributes. The brand has to communicate that what we do is important and that we are special. This organizational brand—I refer to it as the *philosophy*—is critical to attracting and keeping "volunteer" employees because they are looking for meaning at work. This is especially true because many institutions that used to provide meaning to people, such as government, family, communities, and even religious institutions, are losing their impact (more on this in Chapter 11).

Make Work Fun

If it's fun, it gets done. Ask yourself: "Are my team members having fun yet? Better yet, ask them. You see, it's hard to get employees to behave like volunteers when work is a big pain. Ask five of your team members to serve on a "Celebration Team." Give them a budget. If you don't have any money, suggest that they contact local merchants who'd love to achieve greater visibility in your company. Ask those merchants to make donations to your Celebration Team, for example, movie tickets, a weekend for two at a local resort, and so on. Just be sure to give those who donate lots of visibility. Now ask the Celebration Team to get together to identify specific things it is planning to do each month that are fun. Tell the team that anything goes, provided that the team stays within its allocated budget and does not violate any laws, rules, or regulations.

Position People to Build on Their Strengths

Statistics tell us that 25 percent of the U.S. population hates what they do, another 56 percent could take it or leave it, and only 19 percent love what they do. Typically, people who love what they do—"volunteers"—are in jobs that let them build on their strengths. So find out what your team members love to do, and do everything in your power to place them in those positions.

Invest in Career Development

If you want your organization to get better, your employees have to get better. This may be common sense, but my experience as a management consultant demonstrates time and time again that common sense is not very common. The best of the 100 best companies to work for in 2001 and 2002—Stockbroker Edward Jones of St. Louis—has got this figured out. This company provided 146 hours of training, 3.8 percent of its payroll, for every employee during 2002. And new brokers get—are you ready for this—*four* times as much training.[5] And in today's economy, where job loyalty has all but vanished, providing valuable training to your employees is about the only fail-safe strategy left to ensure that "volunteers" stay with you. This is so because employees who feel that they are growing on the job are much more likely to feel like volunteers and stick with you.

Pay Well and Provide Generous Benefits

"But we can't afford that" is what I am told repeatedly, especially by managers who have high turnover rates. So let's do a little bit of quick math. Let's assume that your turnover rate is 25 percent, your average salary including benefits is $40,000 per year per employee, and you have 200 employees. Human resources professionals estimate that replacing an experienced employee costs—depending on skill level—an average of one to one and a half times the employees' annual salary. Some of this cost is obvious, such as recruiting, interviewing, and training costs. The greatest proportion, however, consists of hidden costs. For example, when you lose an experienced employee, customer satisfaction will be lowered, which may have a significant negative impact on your bottom line. And the new employee, even when trained properly, will not perform at the same level of competence and productivity as an experienced employee for at least several months. This, too, costs you. In addition, there are many other hidden costs every time you lose an experienced employee. Let's be conservative and use the one times annual salary estimate. This means that the turnover cost for this hypothetical case is $2 million per year (50 employees × $40,000). If you are able to cut the turnover rate in half, you would save $1 million per year. I bet that even if you paid slightly more than the competition, tied additional compensation to performance such as customer satisfaction, and provided your employees with highly valued fringe benefits, you would have lots of money left over—money that would go straight to your bottom line.

Help Employees Succeed

You know the old saw: Nothing breeds success like success. Well, guess what, it's true. "Volunteers" want to feel good about themselves, and one of the best ways to do this is to help them succeed faster. So promote from within, and do whatever you can to provide team members with highly challenging assignments. Provide tuition assistance, empower, coach, and do whatever it takes to enable team members to succeed, and while they are doing that, they will just happen to make significant contributions to the overall success of your organization. That's nice!

Build a High-Trust Workplace

High trust starts with telling employees more than they want to know, making sure that your word is as good as gold, and giving employees self-confidence so that they can become the best they can be. And it's supplemented with a strong bias against layoffs. (Edward Jones and a great majority of the 100 best companies have never had a mass layoff. More on this in Chapter 13.)

Be Positive and Energetic

Attitudes, just like colds, are catching. Positive attitudes are caught just as easily as negative attitudes. The only problem is that negative attitudes suck the energy out of your team members like a giant sponge—something "volunteers" are just not going to put up with. On the other hand, positive attitudes are like the little Energizer bunny. They'll keep your team members going, and going, and going (well, you get it). To build a positive attitude, become aware of your conversations, including the ones that you have inside your head. Recognize that positive language energizes you and that negative, cynical, "stinking thinking" conversations deenergize you and your team members. Make it a practice to say positive things, especially about other people, or say nothing at all. Also recognize that your mind can hold only one thought at a time. It can either be positive or negative—it is your choice! So, when you catch yourself thinking positive thoughts, congratulate yourself. On the other hand, when you are thinking negative thoughts, catch yourself, change those thoughts, and then give yourself credit. Remember that your team members take their cue from you. You must be the role model for the kinds of behaviors you want them to exhibit. (For in-depth strategies on how to make this happen, read *Make It a Winning Life*.[6])

What's all this add up to? My work with highly successful companies has shown me that treating your team members like volunteers means that you will have lower turnover rates, will be able to pick the cream of the crop any time you need to fill a vacancy, and will achieve massive improvements in your overall profitability.

Smile

The boss was complaining in the all-hands meeting that he wasn't getting any respect. Later he went to a local novelty shop and bought a decorative sign that read, "I'm the Boss," which he taped to his office door. The next day he found that someone had stuck a "sticky note" to the sign that read, "Your wife called. She wants her sign back!"

SMART STEPS

Don't be a glutton. This chapter has more *smart steps* than you can handle. So what are you waiting for? Get started right *now!*

Don't Focus on the Bottom Line

*Using profitability to drive your company is like driving a car by look-
ing in the rearview mirror.*

—WOLF J. RINKE

JUST ABOUT EVERY COMPANY I have ever consulted with was, first and foremost, focused on the bottom line. Some said they weren't. They said that
their customers came first. Others said that their employees were their most
valuable resource. But then comes truth or consequences, which is revealed
when you attend their staff meeting. What is the first thing on the agenda?
What takes up the great majority of the meeting time? Is it customer or
employee satisfaction? Is it the mission, vision, or core values? Or is it the
humongous overarching goal (HOG)? Nope—it's the numbers. (At least a
public company has a partial excuse. After all, investors have a very short
attention span, and all they want to know about is the numbers.) But it is
equally true of private companies. (Don't be so smug about it. Get real and
evaluate what you are spending most of your time on?) And the problem
is that if you spend most of your time focusing on the bottom line, you are
driving a car by looking in the rearview mirror. The financials give you
very little information about how your "car" has reached its destination

or about the obstacles that are in your way. (By the way, there is a reason why your car's front window is much bigger than your rearview mirror.)

In other words, being in business is somewhat like a game of football. If you want to win, you have to focus on the ball—your customers, employees, philosophy (mission, vision, and core values), and your HOG (see Chapter 12). And if you and your team members do this consistently and passionately and hang in there for the long term, the bottom line will take care of itself. (Most of the time when I share this with executives, they declare me insane or tell me that I "just don't understand.") On the other hand, if you spend all your time looking at the scoreboard—the bottom line—you will lose track of the ball and certainly lose the game. Just as in a game of football, you need to define the playing field and have a goal and a game plan.

The playing field—letting your team members know when they are in or out, that is, being safe versus getting in trouble—can be defined in a variety of ways. You can do it with policies and procedures. This seems logical, but in fact, it's bad stuff. It will make you sluggish and nonresponsive to customer needs. (You know how it goes—"It's not in my job description.") Most important, you simply are not innovative enough to anticipate all the ways that people will screw up. And if you do, the number of policies and procedures will bury you. Besides, when was the last time that an employee came running into your office exclaiming, "Boss, I have a customer service problem. Where is the policies and procedures manual?"

What's left? A mission, vision, and core values statement that guides team members' behaviors and actions. There is a problem, though.

Mission Statements Do Not Work

Well, at least now I have your attention. Mission statements, corporate vision statements, or philosophy statements—just about every company has one, yet very few have figured out how to make them come alive—how to define corporate values that truly guide employees' actions and motivate them to extraordinary performance.

Case in point: The managers of a high-tech company hired me to help them define the company's mission, vision, and core values—what I collectively call a *corporate philosophy*. I took the executive team on a two-day retreat and crafted a brief, memorable, passionate document that reflected the purpose of the company, where they saw the company going, and the ideals they would never compromise. The next step was implementation. Despite my recommendation, they insisted that they could accomplish this on their own. The system I prescribed, however, got short-changed. And one more step, probably the most important— install an execution strategy to keep everyone accountable—got left out all together.

A year later the CEO asked me to come back for damage control. It seemed like he just couldn't get everyone to "sing from the same sheet of music." Over lunch I quizzed him regarding the mission, vision, and core values. He had no clue. He wanted everyone to move in the same direction but couldn't express what that direction was supposed to be.

This is an exception, you say. Think again. In company after company I see mission statements that are worthless pieces of paper that cost their weight in gold. Or worse, they spawn widespread cynicism. Once you commit something to paper, it defines a set of aspirations that you must live by. If you don't, employees become disillusioned and demoralized, causing a *reduction* in employee morale and productivity. It's like going to a well-known retailer who touts in its advertising that it "delivers superior customer service." Once you get there, however, there is no employee to be found. And those you do find seem to be from Mars. I don't know about you. I'm out the door, never to return.

So what am I saying? Don't bother with this mission, vision, and core values? No, not at all. If you do it right, it will pay you back handsomely. According to research conducted by Success Profiles, which divided 600 companies into three groups in accordance with how effectively they used their mission, vision, and guiding principles to drive their business, employees in companies that rated "poor" in the use of this business practice generated an average profit of $7802 per employee. Those which rated "average" generated $16,152 per employee, whereas those which were the "best" at using their organizational philosophy generated an average profit of $27,401 per employee.[1]

How to Make Your Philosophy Work for You

Step 1. Get Real

Are you and your leadership team passionate about building a positive corporate culture? Are you prepared to define your mission (what is our primary purpose?), vision (what we want the company to be when it grows up), and core values (what we will *never* compromise—even if they became a competitive *dis*advantage)? Note the emphasis is on the word *never* because if it is changeable, it is not a core value. Are you willing to make them public? And here comes the real big question: Are you committed to walk the talk; that is, are each of you prepared to demonstrate what you profess with your *actions* all the time? Are you willing to commit the time and resources not only to define your philosophy but also to hang in there for the long term to make it part of your culture? If the answer is "No" to any of these, quit right here. Go about doing business as you currently are. At least your team members won't consider you a hypocrite. If you said "Yes" to all, read the example that follows, and then go on to the next step.

Want a great role model? Look at the Johnson & Johnson credo (Exhibit 11-1) defined in 1943 by Robert Wood Johnson II. The wordy manifesto of moral obligations was *mandated* by General Johnson—you either committed to abide by the Johnson & Johnson credo or you could look for work elsewhere. It was that simple and yet that complex. It was simple because it provided incredible results for Johnson & Johnson. For example, during the 31 years that General Johnson managed the company, he expanded his father's business from about $15 million in sales to $500 million. Today, Johnson & Johnson is the thirty-fourth largest company on the Fortune 500 list with over $36 billion in revenues.[2]

It is complex because living the Johnson & Johnson philosophy requires constant and costly recommitment. It starts with the credo being posted in every facility around the world and carved in an eight-foot rock of limestone at the company's headquarters in New Brunswick, New Jersey. It continues with James Burke, former CEO of Johnson & Johnson, convening his executive team in 1979 and saying to them, "Here is the credo. If we're not going to live by it, let's tear it off the wall."[3] After a hearty debate, Burkes' executive team recommitted themselves to living the credo and in a trickle-down manner conducted similar recommitment meetings all over the world. This certainly was an expensive and challenging initiative that somehow seems like a luxury in today's rapidly moving and highly competitive world. Or is it? To get the answer, you have to fast forward three years to 1982—the Tylenol crisis, when Burke was advised by all the powers that be, including his board of directors, the federal government, and

Exhibit 11-1 *The Johnson & Johnson Credo*

Our Credo

We believe our first responsibility is to the doctors, nurses and patients,
to mothers and fathers and all others who use our products and services.
In meeting their needs everything we do must be of high quality.
We must constantly strive to reduce our costs
in order to maintain reasonable prices.
Customers' orders must be serviced promptly and accurately.
Our suppliers and distributors must have an opportunity
to make a fair profit.
We are responsible to our employees,
the men and women who work with us throughout the world.
Everyone must be considered as an individual.
We must respect their dignity and recognize their merit.
They must have a sense of security in their jobs.
Compensation must be fair and adequate,
and working conditions clean, orderly and safe.
We must be mindful of ways to help our employees fulfill
their family responsibilities.
Employees must feel free to make suggestions and complaints.
There must be equal opportunity for employment, development
and advancement for those qualified.
We must provide competent management,
and their actions must be just and ethical.
We are responsible to the communities in which we live and work
and to the world community as well.
We must be good citizens – support good works and charities
and bear our fair share of taxes.
We must encourage civic improvements and better health and education.
We must maintain in good order
the property we are privileged to use,
protecting the environment and natural resources.
Our final responsibility is to our stockholders.
Business must make a sound profit.
We must experiment with new ideas.
Research must be carried on, innovative programs developed
and mistakes paid for.
New equipment must be purchased, new facilities provided
and new products launched.
Reserves must be created to provide for adverse times.
When we operate according to these principles,
the stockholders should realize a fair return.

Johnson & Johnson

Source: *http://www.jnj.com/our_company/our_credo/;* accessed August 6, 2003.
Courtesy Johnson & Johnson.

others, not to pull Tylenol off the shelf. The board didn't want to incur the cut of roughly $100 million in earnings plus the loss of market share. The government did not want to encourage copycats. Instead of listening to that advice, Burke revisited the credo, which clearly stated in the first lines: "We believe our first responsibility is to the doctors, nurses and patients, to mothers and fathers and all others who use our products and services" (see Exhibit 11-1). This same contrarian approach was replicated once again by Burke in 1986. The bottom-line result: Instead of the dire consequences predicted, Johnson & Johnson's reputation was preserved, and the Tylenol business was regained.[4]

Step 2. Define a Philosophy That Will Serve as a Blueprint for Team Members' Behavior

Reach consensus with your senior executive team—this is *not* an all-hands process—regarding your mission, vision, and core values. (Heck, if you are the CEO, you can do this on your own—that's what General Johnson did.) Get them away from the day-to-day interruptions, and don't go home until it's done. An effective facilitator can help you get this accomplished in one and a half to two days. (I happen to know someone like that—guess who?) Whatever you do, stay away from motherhood and apple pie politically correct statements, especially when it comes to core values. For example, what do you think about the following core values? Respect. Integrity. Excellence. This is great stuff, right? They are short, concise, and memorable. They meet all the requirements of great core values, right? Think again! These were Enron's core values.

Instead, identify ethics-based core values even if they seem to work against short-term results. For example, The Container Store, Tom's of Maine, and Southwest Airlines are finding that operating by an ethics-based organizational philosophy is increasing employee satisfaction and improving the bottom line. For example, The Container Store stresses to its employees that they are ". . . morally obligated to help customers solve problems and not just sell them products." The company has achieved sales increases of 20 to 25 percent since opening its first store in 1978.[5] Also, don't fret about the format of your philosophy. In fact, Johnson & Johnson's credo breaks all the rules. It's a 310-word credo that most people would find difficult to memorize or recall. However, they make it work.

Remember, the magic is *not* in having a philosophy or having it in the right format, the magic is *living it!*

Step 3. Get Buy-In

You must strive for critical mass—which means that you must get buy-in from at least two-thirds of all employees. And the only way that this will happen is to involve them in the process. I achieve buy-in by conducting an organization-wide slogan contest that involves every employee. (For details and samples, see Chapter 2 in *Winning Management: 6 Fail-Safe Strategies for Building High Performance Organizations*, by yours truly.[6])

Step 4. Make the Philosophy Come Alive

Reinforce the philosophy with your own actions. Want a great role model? Think of Sir Richard Branson of the Virgin Group in the United Kingdom, who is the founder of one of the most successful businesses in the United Kingdom, an extraordinary brand builder, and an adventurer—sailing and ballooning around the world. One of his core values is that work should be fun. And he lives it. Branson's autobiography is entitled, *Losing My Virginity*. He put on a bridal dress to launch his new company Virgin Bridal and launched Virgin Mobile in New York City almost buck naked—okay, so he had on a body stocking. And even though Branson manages 224 companies—mostly privately held—he devotes an extraordinary amount of time to his wife Joan and their two teenage children—all the while having an extraordinary amount of fun and insisting that all the people who work with him do the same thing. The way that Branson says it is: "I don't think of work as work and play as play. It's all living."[7] Always make sure that you *live* the philosophy so that you can help your team members do the same. When coaching, counseling, or evaluating employees, ask them to assess how their own actions and behaviors help to move the company closer to achieving *our* philosophy.

Step 5. Overcommunicate the Philosophy

In addition to living the philosophy, talk about your mission, vision, or core values at least six times every day to someone. The day that you're getting sick and tired of talking about it is the day that your team members will begin to internalize the philosophy. For example, Johnson & Johnson revisits the credo virtually every year with all team members. Today, the credo lives on stronger than ever. Over the years, some of the language of the credo has been updated, and new areas recognizing the environment and the balance between work and family have been added. However, the spirit of the document remains the same today as when it was first written some 50 years ago.

Step 6. Put Teeth into It

Teeth are the specific benchmarks or metrics that transform the philosophy into reality. Get all employees involved in this process. Then set up a tracking system that ensures that everyone is singing from the same sheet of music. Make all this information public to implement peer power and to keep everyone on their toes. And whatever you do, keep it simple. Remember, *less is more*.

Step 7. Install an Execution Strategy and Feedback Loop

Since this is the step that in my experience is most often omitted, let me share a few specific examples. For example, Johnson & Johnson employees participate in a periodic survey and evaluation of just how well the company performs its credo responsibilities. These assessments are then fed back to the senior management team, and where there are shortcomings, corrective action is taken. Granite Rock, Inc., is in the unglamorous business of selling crushed gravel, concrete, sand, and asphalt. The company's vision is "Granite Rock will provide total customer satisfaction and achieve a reputation for service that meets or exceeds that of Nordstrom." (Did you catch that? The company is selling gravel and wants to be like Nordstrom. This is a *wow* in my book!) The way the company keeps itself on track is with what it calls "short pay." The bottom of every invoice says: "If you are not satisfied for any reason, don't pay us for it. Simply scratch out the line item, write a brief note about the problem, and return a copy of this invoice along with your check for the balance." As a result of this contrarian strategy, Granite Rock continues to gain market share, even though it charges a 6 percent premium price and achieves a pretax return of about 10 percent. This is not bad for selling "stones."[8]

Step 8. Celebrate

This is another biggie. Share the glory and wealth, and have fun. Remember, *if it's fun, it gets done.*

Step 9. Live It

This is the most important of all the steps and the only one that will lead to disaster if you violate it. Check your organizational philosophy using the check sheet in Exhibit 11-2.

Exhibit 11-2 *Philosophy Check Sheet*

Our mission describes
____ What we are in business for.
____ What products/services we provide.
____ What our products/services will do for our customers.
____ What sets us apart from the competition.

Our vision describes
____ Our dream for the future (what we want to be when we grow up).
____ A journey not a destination.
____ What is unique about us.
____ What our real priorities are for the next 10 to 30 years.
____ What we want to accomplish that will cause most team members to be committed, aligned, and proud to be part of this organization/company.

Our *core* values describe
____ What is important to us (what we will *never* compromise even if it becomes a competitive *dis*advantage).

Other:
____ It's short, to the point, passionate, and memorable.
____ It has no more than five core values.
____ It fits on one page

Most important:
____ *Every member of the leadership team "lives" the philosophy!*
(Even if you don't do any of the above, this one is nonnegotiable.)

Smile

Comment made by a Southwest Airline flight attendant: "The reason why we are a bit late today is that it is taking the baggage handlers longer than normal to rip the handles off your luggage."

SMART STEPS

Tomorrow, walk into your organization as if it were for the first time and as if you were a team member. Count the number of times you see the philosophy statement before you get to your place of work. If it is fewer than three times, get your philosophy statement printed on laminated posters and distribute them in high-traffic areas throughout your organization. Imprint it on your pens, paychecks, stationery, customer literature, and anywhere else you can think of.

Take every opportunity to communicate the philosophy. If you are not sharing it with someone at least six times each working day, you are not doing your job. Don't worry about too much repetition. You *can't* overdo it.

The next time you have an occasion to coach one of your team members, use your philosophy statement to guide your coaching.

Make sure that your philosophy guides all your major decisions, such as competitive strategies, acquisitions, hiring and firing, promotions, and so on.

During your next team meeting when people get sidetracked with petty interpersonal issues, ask them: "How will the resolution of this issue help us get closer to the attainment of our mission or vision?" If they are unable to tell you how, ask: "Do you feel that this issue deserves our valuable time and attention?"

The next time one of your team members asks you what to do, answer: "What do you think?" If she is not sure how to answer the question, ask her what document she could use to help guide her decision.

Look for team members relying on the organization's philosophy statement to make decisions. Then let them know how impressed you are.

Don't Have Goals and Objectives

The greater danger is not that our hopes are too high and we fail to reach them. It's that they are too low, and we do.

—MICHELANGELO

IN CHAPTER 11 YOU LEARNED HOW TO DEFINE the playing field and identify the vision for your organization. Your team members also need a goal to shoot for. To accomplish this, I recommend that you get *one* humongous overarching goal (HOG) that drives employees' energies in laserlike fashion in a singular direction for the next 10 to 30 years and makes your vision come alive.

Here are a couple of examples. The year was 1940, and a gentleman by the name of Charles E. Merrill, standing in an office in New York not much bigger than a closet, shared his HOG with his *two* employees: "Merrill Lynch will be one of the finest and most profitable financial services company with offices all around the world." Today, Merrill Lynch has offices in 43 countries, assets of close to $448 billion, and over 50,000 employees. And even though Merrill Lynch was negatively affected by the bursting of the tech stock bubble and 9/11, it is still number 48 on the Fortune 500 list of the largest U.S. corporations.[1]

Another example is Sam Walton's "We will be a $125 billion company by the year 2000," a statement he made in 1990 and a vision that was achieved even without Sam's charisma by his successor, David Glass. In fact, in 2000 Wal-Mart had grown to $165 billion, and today it is *the* largest company in the *world*, with over $246 billion in revenues in 2002. Other examples include "We will be number 1 or 2 in every market we serve . . . and have the strength of a big company with the leanness and agility of a small company," a vision that Jack Welch made a reality during his tenure at General Electric (GE). And then, of course, there was President John Kennedy's HOG during a joint session of Congress on May 25, 1961: "I believe that this nation should commit itself to achieving the goal, before this decade is out, to land a man on the moon and returning him safely to the Earth." And even though that HOG, like all effective HOGs, was derided by the skeptics as an impossible dream and by others as lunacy, Kennedy's dream became a reality on July 20, 1969, when Neil Armstrong took "a small step for a man and a giant leap for mankind." In fact, a total of 12 Apollo astronauts would reach the moon surface from 1969 to 1972.

Are you wondering: "Why only one HOG? Hey, if one is good, why not 3, 5, or 12?" Remember the old days of management by objectives (MBO)? Basically, managers learned how to look good—they identified all kinds of objectives—easy ones so that they could prove just how much they had accomplished. In other words, they got really good at majoring in minors. And before you knew it, MBO became a monster that needed to be fed and taken care of so that a good portion of managers' time was taken up by feeding the monster. The result? Managers had really great looking "objectives" but didn't get much done. (Notice that in football you shoot only at one goal. Unless you're all confused and score points for the opposition, which, of course, some managers do.)

A HOG with teeth, meaning that you have specific measurement systems (metrics) in place that track progress, on the other hand, tends to focus various parts of an organization on creating strategic alignment and big results. For example, from research conducted by Morgan and Rao, who refer to this as "Super-Measure Management" (SMM),[2] the new CEO of Continental Airlines, Gordon Bethune, used SMM to stop Continental from hemorrhaging cash. In 1994 when he took the reigns, Continental had lost an average of $960 million per year for four years in a row, its stock was trading at $5 per share, customers perceived Continental as unreliable, and employees were highly dissatisfied—not just dissatisfied, employees distrusted management and each other, back stabbing and blaming was the order of the day, and pride in the company was nonexistent. To effect a dramatic turnaround, Bethune focused every employee's energy on one HOG: Improve our on-time performance ranking from being last to rank among the top three airlines. To sweeten the deal, he announced in 1995 that anytime Continental was among the top three major airlines in on-time performance, he would pay every nonmanagement employee $65 extra per month. One month after that offer, Continental had moved from being last to first in the on-time rankings, as measured by the Department of Transportation. Bethune paid the $65 that month and continued paying it six more times in 1995. The on-time HOG focused the energies of all employees so well that by 2000 Continental was ranked number one in on-time arrivals among all major U.S. airlines. During that year, every employee received an average of $785 in on-time bonuses. The spin-off benefit was that Continental was also rated number one in customer satisfaction.

How to Make Your HOG Come Alive

Step 1. Define Your Strategic Direction

If you defined your vision, that is, what you want to be when your company grows up, you've got this done (see Chapter 11). When doing this, remember to apply the KISS principle aggressively—Keep it Simple Smarty.

Step 2. Define Your HOG

Make sure that you pick only one really humongous overarching goal (HOG) that defines the direction of your organization for the next 10 to 30 years, that it has only about a 50 to 75 percent probability of success, and that everyone in your organization from executives to frontline employees can directly or indirectly have an impact on it. Your team members have no reason to stretch if they can't influence the outcome. If you can't figure out what the HOG should be, identify a humongous overarching customer satisfaction goal because everyone has a customer, and everyone can have an impact on customer satisfaction measurements. An obvious but often overlooked strategy is to involve as many of your team members as possible in defining the HOG. Involvement buys ownership, and ownership achieves results faster.

Step 3. Establish Benchmarks and a Tracking System

Achieving a HOG can be an extremely long-term process—10 to 30 years in this highly competitive global economy is an eternity. So you need a tracking system that monitors progress to let team members know how well they are doing. For example, Continental measured achievement of their HOG—on-time performance ranking among the top three airlines—on a monthly basis. If you can't come up with a monthly metric, and I don't see why not, then you will need to identify interim benchmarks that are widely understood by all team members, measurable, and tied directly to attainment of the HOG.

Step 4. Develop an Incentive System That Is Tied to Attainment of the HOG

I call this a *humongous incredible reward* (HIR). In an ideal world, the reward system should be a combination of external (e.g., money) and internal (e.g., sense of satisfaction) rewards. If in doubt, be more generous than you think is wise. And be sure that awards and incentives are important to your team members. For example, don't be like one of the nursing homes I consulted with in Chicago. It offered a free parking space as one of its incentives. Unfortunately, this did not mean much to most employees. Why? Because most of them used public transportation. How can you figure out what people really want? Are you ready for a startling revelation? *You ask them!* Or better yet, you involve them by inviting employees to become members of an "awards and incentive team." Give the team a name—the "HIR Team"—and a budget, and watch it create magic. Be sure to have individuals and teams compete against themselves or against standards. Avoid having people compete against each other within the same organization. The reason: If there is a winner, there will be a loser. Losing demoralizes people, and demoralized people are less productive and are more likely to quit. And if at all possible, track and recognize the performance of individuals, teams, and the entire organization. Remember: *Whatever you reward is what you get.*

Step 4. Communicate and Educate

Any time you are attempting to change anything in your organization, you have to tell people more than they want to know and tell them more often than you think is wise. And, oh yes, use every available medium when doing this. When distributing status reports, make liberal use of charts and graphs. Remember, a picture is worth a thousand words. And if the members of you organization don't understand it—no, they are not dumb; *you* have not explained it very well. And be sure to make performance information public. Yes, both the good and the bad. Just exercise double caution to make sure that your information is accurate, especially any negative information. When the enthusiasm wanes, it's time for more communication. Encourage and reward team members for sharing best practices that contribute to attainment of the HOG. You also will need to educate certain team members such as administration folks and other support personnel regarding how their efforts contribute to attainment of the HOG in a very important, albeit indirect, manner.

My experience shows that when it comes to communication, many leaders just don't get it. For example, in most companies I have worked with, the employees felt like they were treated like mushrooms. The way you do this is you keep them in the dark and feed them nothing but manure (you get my drift). Since you seem to be puffed up—pun intended—with righteous indignation, let me take you on a journey to make my point.

Imagine for a moment that it is early January, and you and 12 other managers from your company have been assembled at an elegant beach resort in the Bahamas. After opening comments from the CEO, I am introduced. The CEO tells you that I have a special project for you and that as soon as that project is completed, all of us get the rest of the day to do whatever we want—swim, sail, scuba dive, or whatever else our hearts desire. Can you smell the ocean, hear the waves lapping on the shore, taste the ice-cold margaritas, and see the sparkling crystal clear water? And, oh yes, it is an absolutely gorgeous day outside. After briefly energizing you—not that you need much of that after those remarks—I give each of you a big handful of puzzle pieces from a plastic bag. Then I tell you that, as a group, you have all the pieces needed to complete the puzzle and that just as soon as you have put it together, we can frolic on the beach. What would you ask for? If you said, "The box top from the puzzle," you would have given the same response I get from most audience members. What you need to get this done in a reasonable time is the box top. Now let me have you pause and think about your team members. Are they asked, like employees in most organizations, to put the puzzle together—to accomplish their work and achieve the HOG—without the box top—without the big picture?

Step 5. Walk Your Talk

Aren't you getting kind of tired of hearing this? You and the senior executive team need to demonstrate passionately your commitment to the HOG by showing team members what you and the leadership team are doing to support achievement of the HOG and by talking about the heroes who have gone beyond the call of duty to contribute to attainment of the HOG.

Step 6. Get Rid of Roadblocks

Engage your team members in conversations regarding what stands in their way of achieving the HOG. You can do this when you are practicing management by walking around (MBWA), organize town hall meetings, have breakfast with the boss, and at any other time that you can engage your employees in conversation. Be sure to listen actively—this is something that's *really* tough to do—take notes, and most important, take action. And then report back to your team members to let them know what you have done. And if you can't do something, tell them that too and the reason why. While I'm talking about roadblocks, also get rid of the procedures manual. Instead, give your team what Eric Rylberg, the CEO of ISS—the Danish global service giant—calls a "license to act." Okay, you don't have to get rid of all of it. Keep what's required by law, but no more. Policies and procedures are progress killers and will get in the way of achieving the HOG.

Step 7. Change the HOG as Necessary

Unlike core values, which never change—otherwise, they are not *core* values—you should be willing to modify the HOG. Let's say that the HOG was to open 500 new stores every year—which was Starbucks' goal—and you are finding that that is a "no-brainer." Change it to become "the most recognized brand worldwide—on par with Coca Cola—which is what Starbucks is working toward.

Step 8. Celebrate More—and More
Often Than You Think Is Wise

A big HOG needs a big HIR (see the Phillips story below). Make sure that you celebrate incremental attainment of the HOG. HOGs, by their very nature, take a long time to achieve, and you need to continue to keep your team members fired up, especially if you are unable to reward them financially for their contributions—as is the case in many government organizations. All human beings move themselves in the direction of pleasure and move away from pain. (Sigmund Freud called this the "pleasure principle.") Thus, if you have trouble keeping your great team members engaged in pursuit of the HOG, ask yourself and them how much fun they are having doing it. Having fun is what this is all about. So do it up right and do it as often as possible. Do it in front of team members, and be sure that the rewards are proportionate to the achievements. If the energy wanes, it's time for more celebration, more pep rallies, and more fun. Remember: *If it's fun, it gets done.*

The Phillips Story

Tom Phillips had a dream—what I call a HOG. He wanted to be the biggest newsletter publisher in the world. Therefore, in 1974 he started Phillips Publishing in his garage. (Don't you ever wonder how businesses would get started without garages?) In 1990 Tom established his second HOG—$100 million in annual sales by 1993. This HOG was supplemented with a HIR: If we achieve the HOG, all Phillips team members and their families will get to go to an all-expense-paid trip to Disney World. The HOG was achieved in 1993, and 1350 Phillips team members, spouses, children, and guests went to Disney World. You can't afford to do anything that lavish, you say. Consider this: The 1993 trip generated a considerable amount of publicity in both local and national media outlets. Some of the highlights included an article in the *Washington Post,* an appearance on the "Today Show," and a mention in the *National Enquirer*—I know you can do without that one—as well as local television coverage of a special Disney Day Celebration held shortly before the trip to build excitement plus much, much more. (Would you care to guess what this level of publicity is worth?)

Tom, now the chairman and president of Phillips International, however, did not stop there. His third HOG was to achieve $300 million in annual sales by 2003. As before, the HOG was supplemented with a HIR—an all-expense-paid, three-night Disney cruise for all team and family members. As a result of achieving this HOG, Phillips is, at the time of this writing, one of the largest newsletter publishers in the world with annual sales of $300 million, and Tom took his employees and their families—over 1300 people—on that promised Disney cruise during the summer of 2003.

I might add that the fun and entrepreneurial spirit are nurtured at Phillips year round. The company holds monthly recognition days, where colleagues are recognized for their birthdays, promotions, and company anniversaries. The company has an "Employee Spirit Team" that organizes events throughout the year that allow colleagues to socialize and contribute to the local community; a bake-off competition; a "Spirit of Giving" event, where colleagues provide nonperishable food items for local homeless shelters; and trivia contests geared around specific holidays, such as Flag Day. In fact, Tom's mantra is, "At Phillips, we work hard and play hard."

Exhibit 12-1 will enable you to check your progress.

Exhibit 12-1 HOG Check Sheet

Does your humongous overarching goal (HOG) describe a huge, daunting challenge that

_____ Is energizing—gets team members' juices flowing?

_____ Creates a clear image in people's minds?

_____ Requires little or no explanation?

_____ Engages your team members' emotions?

_____ Is tangible?

_____ Is clear, concise, and to the point?

_____ Is compelling?

_____ Is tied to an incentive system that all employees can affect?

_____ Has a 50 to 75 percent probability of success over the next 10 to 30 years?

_____ Is perceived as feasible by at least two-thirds of team members?

_____ Will serve as a unifying force?

_____ Moves you closer to the attainment of your vision?

_____ Describes a clear finish line?

_____ Instills passion and commitment in at least two-thirds of team members?

_____ Is supported by a HIR that keeps team members motivated?

Smile

Excerpt from an employee manual:

Restroom Use

Entirely too much time is being spent in the restroom. In the future, we will follow the practice of going in alphabetical order. For instance, all employees whose names begin with A will go from 8:00 to 8:20, employees whose names begin with B will go from 8:20 to 8:40, and so on. If you're unable to go at your allotted time, it will be necessary to wait until the next day when your turn comes again. In extreme emergencies employees may swap their time with a coworker. Both employees' supervisors must approve this exchange in writing. In addition, there is now a strict three-minute time limit in the stalls. At the end of three minutes, an alarm will sound, the toilet paper roll will retract, and the stall door will open.

SMART STEPS

Randomly select about 10 percent of the team members who work with you. (Note: People work *with* you—*not for* you!) Make sure that you select at least one individual from each section or department. Visit each team member during the next month, and ask him what the HOG is. If 95 percent or more of the team members can describe the essence of the HOG, you are doing great. If not, make up an action plan to communicate and educate.

Take every opportunity to communicate the HOG. If you are not sharing it with someone at least six times each working day, you are not doing your job. Don't worry about too much repetition. You *can't* overdo it.

Continued

Continued

Find out what is getting in your team members' way of contributing to the HOG by spending at least a third of your time with them.

Consistently practice what you teach. Remember that actions speak louder than words and that what is important to you tends to be important to your *valuable* team members.

Get excited about the HOG, and be sure to spread that excitement to all your team members and customers. If you can't get excited about the HOG, change it.

Challenge your leadership team to come up with a HIR that gets *national* media attention.

13

Trust All People All the Time

Trust men, and they will be true to you; treat them greatly, and they will show themselves great.

—RALPH WALDO EMERSON

"TRUST ALL PEOPLE ALL THE TIME, until they prove you wrong" is the advice I provide in my seminars and consulting activities. Typical responses are "You don't understand the people who work for me" or "You sure have no clue who our customers are" or "I wouldn't trust my manager if my life depended on it." In one way I understand. After all, trust has become a vanishing act in corporate America. No wonder, with all the mergers, reengineering, layoffs, and the Enron-type debacles, that employees find it increasingly difficult to trust management. According to a study of 1800 employees by Aon's Loyalty Institute of Ann Arbor, Michigan, "13 percent of U.S. workers distrust their employers on the most basic level—they don't feel free from fear, intimidation or harassment at work." In a similar study of more than 7500 employees, Watson Wyatt Worldwide of Bethesda, Maryland, found that "only half trusted senior managers."[1]

Here is the so-what: According to Watson Wyatt, ". . . companies where employees trusted top executives posted shareholder returns 42 percentage points higher than companies where distrust was the rule."[2]

The Corporate Leadership Team Merry-Go-Round

The consequences when leaders do not trust their team members are perhaps best illustrated by the following story (names have been changed to protect the guilty). In 1995, John, the senior vice president of a high-tech company, engaged me. John and Chris, the CEO, president, and owner of the company, wanted me to help them with improving the effectiveness of the senior management team.

My in-depth organizational assessment interviews with all members of the executive team revealed that Chris had lost trust in John and several members of the executive team that John had brought on board. The trust had deteriorated to such a low level that I recommended that John be asked to leave and that the executive team be reorganized. This is exactly what was done—at great expense to the company. Moreover, this was done even though my organizational assessment had revealed that much of the lack of trust resided primarily in *Chris,* the CEO, not John or the management team. That lack of trust had resulted in Chris taking a variety of steps that undermined John and his management team's ability to get the job done. (John had been brought on board because Chris was getting on in years, and the company had grown too large for Chris to handle. John and his highly qualified and expensive leadership team of five executives had been given carte blanche for running the day-to-day affairs of the company.) In other words, Chris had set John and his team up to fail from the start. This is why I strongly urged Chris to allow me to coach him (Chris) to ensure that the next team would be more successful. I also suggested that once the new executive team was on board we conduct an intensive trust-building initiative to get the new leadership team started on the right foot. Chris, however, externalized the problem and hence saw no need to be coached because "John and his team just could not be trusted, and once I get the right team on board, everything will be fine."

About mid-1998 the new team had been brought on board, and, you guessed it, about three years later I got another call from Chris with a request for help that was literally like someone had just rewound the video and let it run all over again. The only thing that had changed was the names of the leadership team members. Once again, trust had deteriorated to such a dysfunctional level that the executive team was asked to leave. And even though this was déjà vu all over again, Chris continued to externalize the problem and once again brought on yet another new executive team. The only change was that Chris held onto the primary responsibility of running the day-to-day affairs of the company himself. It has been just about three years, and I'm expecting a call from Chris anytime now.

Now stop a moment and think of the incredible costs and loss in productivity sustained by this company all because the leader—Chris—is unable to trust people and is unwilling to take ownership of a problem that can only be corrected by affecting changes in himself. And I predict that unless Chris sells the company—this is his baby, and he is unable and unwilling to change—the company ultimately will fail. After all, trust is the foundation on which all relationships and interactions are built. And once that foundation is destroyed, relationships and interactions can no longer function smoothly, effectively, or productively.

Here is the message in a nutshell: If you consistently mistrust all your team members all the time, you will be correct 3 percent of the time. Not very good odds, are they? If, on the other hand, you trust all your people all the time until they prove you wrong, you will be right 97 percent of the time. Why not bet on the much better odds? It is your choice; don't give it away!

So what can you do to build trust in your organization? You can start by invoking the law of reciprocity, which says that *whatever you give is what you're going to get.* (See Chapter 6.) Therefore, if you want more trust, you have to give it first. (And, by the way, all this stuff works at home, too, because we are talking about what it takes to build strong relationships—at work or at home.)

The next thing you can do is make sure that your word is *always* as good as gold, that your team members never have to second-guess anything you tell them, and that they can count on you to do right by them, your customers, and your organization. Once you get the basics down pat, here are six additional steps you can take to build trust in your organization.

Step 1. Hold Everyone Accountable

Always hold all team members accountable for all their actions. One way to do this is to have them commit to this powerful axiom: *If it's to be, it's up to me!* You might even make up a huge poster with those words, followed by, "I hereby commit to take ownership of all my actions," and then have all team members sign the poster. (Remember the law of commitment from Chapter 6?) Once signed, display the poster in a conspicuous place for all customers and team members to see. Also, since it is difficult to establish accountability among more than about 50 people, make sure that you subgroup your organization into small business units of ideally no more than 50 people per group. Typically, people act more responsibly when they are in groups where everyone knows everyone else on a personal level. (This is why it is such a challenge to manage virtual teams.) It prevents *anomie*, the French term that describes a society that is falling apart because normative standards of conduct are weak.

Step 2. Establish Boundaries

Trust works when people know that they can count on each other to do a certain thing a certain way. How things are done in an organization should be defined by the organization's philosophy—but you know that already (see Chapter 11). Once the boundaries are in place, you must then discipline *yourself* to expect that your team members are going to operate within those boundaries. Why? Because over the long term you will get what you expect. Control in such an environment comes *after* the action, when results are assessed, instead of telling people what to do or having them ask permission before taking action. This allows you to function as a coach instead of a cop (see Chapter 16) and makes your team members respect and trust you more.

Step 3. Build a Learning Organization

Trust requires lifelong learning because it can only come about if people can count on each other to perform at peak performance. Such performance is only possible if you have provided people with the resources to engage in lifelong learning and constant renewal and change. To accomplish the latter, you also must give people permission to make mistakes. And the best way to do this is for you to admit *publicly* when you have made a mistake. Once your team members see that you are less than perfect, they too *may* be willing—some people will never reach this level of maturity—to admit it when they have made a mistake. This, in turn, will enable your team members to be willing to take calculated risks and find a better way to do everything all the time and then share both their successes *and* their failures with other team members. In addition, build a learning library of books and audio and video programs that you can use for training purposes and that team members can check out for independent learning so that they can become the best they can be. (Remember, an organization is only as good as its people.) I would especially recommend that you encourage your team members to listen to motivational and educational audio programs on the way to work. In this way they arrive with a turned-on, tuned-in, positive attitude that will enable them to deal more effectively with stress, get along with their team members, and take better care of customers.

Step 4. Practice Tough Love

Highly effective leaders *love* their team members the way they are, not the way they ought to be. (You need to read that again. It took me over 26 years to master, and it's worth the price of this book many times over.) The paradox, of course, is that all of us are like red wine, which means that we have the opportunity to get better all the time. Moreover, contrarian leaders (CLs) help their team members get better all the time, which, of course, requires love. And love is not possible without trust. Therefore, people who *intentionally* and repeatedly abuse trust must be removed from the organization because you must be able to trust all your people all the time. Otherwise, you will revert back to functioning like an autocratic manager—a manager who does the checking and controlling *in advance,* as opposed to operating like a *contrarian leader,* who lets the organizational philosophy do the checking and controlling and only deals with team members who *intentionally* violate that gold standard.

Step 5. Walk Your Talk

I know you've heard this one before, but this is not about hearing it, it's about doing, because trust will only come alive as a result of reinforcing your words with your *actions.* I have my seminar participants prove this to themselves by having everyone stand and look at me and follow my directions. I tell them to extend their right arm, just as I am doing. Next, I tell them to form a circle with their index finger and thumb and place that circle on their cheek. As I say *cheek,* I put my thumb and index finger circle on my *chin.* What happens next is quite comical. Most participants look like they have an early onset of Alzheimer's disease because their arm will tremble as they waver between cheek and chin. Others place the circle on the chin and can't quite understand what the fuss is all about. Typically, only a few participants will follow my clear *verbal* instructions and place the circle on their cheek. Next, I have them look at each other, which results in another salvo of snickers and laughter, and then I have them tell me what happened. Of course, they tell me that they were influenced much more by my *actions* than by my words. The same is true for your team members. This is why you must be the role model of everything that you want to have happen in your organization. And if you don't like that, it's time to get out of leadership and become a consultant like I did. (Sorry, but that is the brutal truth.)

Step 6. Practice High Touch

High tech increasingly will be the norm as we move toward virtual organizations. Without high touch, however, in the form of meetings, organizational retreats, and conferences, trust will wither on the vine. There simply is no shortcut to developing trust with another human being. It can't be done via the Internet, voice mail, faxes, or other electronic media. It requires you to be belly to belly, nose to nose, and eye to eye with another human being so that you can make sure that a person's body language reinforces and supports his words. So be sure to get out of your office and spend quality time with the people who are responsible for 85 percent of your success—your team members.

Smile

A tourist climbed out of his car in downtown Washington. He said to a man who was standing near the curb, "Listen, I'm only going to be gone a couple of minutes. Would you do me a favor and watch my car while I go in the store?"

"What?" the man huffed. "Do you realize that I am a member of the United States Senate?"

"No, I didn't realize that," the tourist said, "but I'm in a hurry, so I guess I'll have to trust you anyway."

SMART STEPS

You have six specific smart steps to implement. What are you waiting for?

14

Don't Oil the Squeaky Wheel

From an employee standpoint, a great place to work is one in which you trust the people you work for, take pride in what you do, and enjoy the people you are working with.

—ROBERT LEVERING

Oiling the Squeaky Wheel in Action

Chief Executive Officer Janice Maloney was at the end of her wits. Her company, consisting of nine offices in the Baltimore-Washington area, I'll call it the Can-Do Mortgage Co (CDM), was falling apart. Sales were down, and this was during the low-interest go-go years where all her competitors were not just thriving but were going through the roof. Employee morale was shot. Her vice presidents were outright depressed. They seemed to be spending more time blaming and avoiding each other than coming up with innovative ideas to solve problems and increase sales. Meetings with her vice presidents, the few she still had, were so negative and downright antagonistic that Janice avoided them like the plague. Yet day after day her calendar was full, responding to requests to meet with employees all the way from vice presidents to frontline employees. Generally, all the meetings seemed to have a common theme. People were blaming, whining, and complaining about each other. What so-and-so did and didn't do. When she did visit with branches—something she knew she had to do, even though she hated it with a passion—people continued the common refrain of blaming, protecting their turf, and generally expressing a sense of helplessness best expressed by Tom, a veteran team member: "This company sucks, everyone bitches about each other, and no one does anything about it!"

Having come to the end of the road, Janice engaged a consultant—all right, so it was me—to find out what was going on. After completing an in-depth organizational assessment, it became very clear to me that Janice had committed a number of leadership follies. One of the biggest was that she had been spending a disproportionate amount of her available time dealing with the troublemakers, the whiners, and the blamers—"oiling the squeaky wheel."

When I went over my findings with Janice, she protested that she had done exactly what she had learned in a leadership program that had advocated the importance of practicing management by walking around (MBWA). "This professor," Janice said, "started his program by asking everyone: 'What business are you in?' He had made it around the room, and executives were saying such things as 'I'm in the real estate business,' '. . . the banking business,' '. . . the automobile business,' and so on. When he got to me, and I was pretty much the last person," Janice said, "I answered, 'I'm in the mortgage business.' At just that point he got really excited and admonished all of us in no uncertain terms, 'All of you have it wrong! You are all in the *people* business—because the minute you assumed management or leadership responsibilities, you gave up being in the mortgage business and chose to be in the people business, because the way you achieve results is not by what you do but rather by what your people do. Since your people are responsible for 85 percent of your success, then it stands to reason that you must spend more time with your people.' " And Janice continued, "Ever since then I've been doing just that, spending more time with my people—visiting branches, establishing an open-door policy, and making myself available to listen to people in small group meetings. I even set up a 'have breakfast with the boss session' on a weekly basis. And ever since I've been doing that," Janice continued, "all I've been hearing is whining, blaming, and complaining." When I asked Janice what she did with the information, she said, "I let people vent, listen very actively, and try to be empathetic. And sometimes I talk to the other party to attempt to get the facts. And that is pretty much it."

At this point I asked Janice to analyze the consequences of her own behavior. When she got stuck, I asked her what the following truism meant to her: *What you reward is what you get.* "You mean to tell me that it is all my fault," she said. "Well," I responded, "not all, but quite a big chunk of it. In other words, you have been 'rewarding' people for doing exactly the things you don't want—whining, blaming, and complaining. And the people who have been taking advantage of that," I continued, "are the people who have lots to whine, blame, and complain about. What about," I then asked her, "your top performers. You know, your high-performing vice presidents, your top salespeople, and your 'water walkers.' How much time have you been spending with them?" Janice looked at me startled. "Actually," she said, "very little. They are my good people—they don't have time to whine, blame, and complain. In fact," Janice said, "ever since I've been listening to the whiners, they've been telling me how overworked and underpaid they are. And so I have been transferring more and more responsibilities to my top performers." (This was a strategy that had truly backfired because more and more of her top performers had left the company.)

"I get it," Janice finally exclaimed somewhat excitedly. "I have been rewarding my troublemakers by giving them a lot of my valuable time. Not only have I not held them accountable, but I also allowed them to unload their worries, complain about their coworkers, and get further rewarded by having more and more work taken away from them."

"Right on," I said. "But what else did you do? What did you do with your top performers?" "I ignored them," said Janice. "Actually, you did much worse than that," I responded. "You 'punished' them, first, by shifting more responsibilities and work to them and, second, by ignoring them." "The professor's advice was really good," I said, "provided that you spend more time with the people who make you look great and spend less time with the trouble makers—the squeaky wheels."

Time for a Reality Check

Now don't sit there all smug, thinking that you never do anything like that. Let's find out if you do. Quick, grab your calendar, may it be electronic or hard copy. Now figure out what proportion of your time you spent with troublemakers and slackers during the past four weeks. If you spent more than 5 percent of your time with troublemakers, you are messing up. If you want your team members to be positive, trusting, turned on, and tuned in, then you must spend the majority of your time with the people who behave that way and, while they are doing it, help you succeed faster. What about the troublemakers—the squeaky wheels? Glad you asked, because I love to share a sure-fire *smart step* with you that will enable you to address this more effectively than ever before.

Here it is: Place the strengths and weaknesses of questionable team members on a balance beam scale. If the weaknesses *consistently* outweigh the strengths, and any type of assistance such as training and coaching seem to have made no measurable difference, it's time to take other actions. First, reassign the squeaky wheels (SWs) to an area that potentially could enable them to build on their strengths. (Please note that I am *not* telling you to reassign them just to get them out of your hair—that's just another way reinforcing the behavior you *don't* want. Think about it: If I screw up long enough, I get sent to a cushy job where no one keeps an eye on me. What a deal.) If this does not work or there is no other place to assign SWs, it's time to take drastic action—that's right, fire them. Better yet, send SWs to the competition. (If you are not smiling, read that again. And if it still does not make you at least grin, it's time to take a break.) Whatever you do, expend the least amount of resources, energy, and time on your SWs.

Smile

Since I just talked about firing someone, here are several phrases you may wish to use the next time you have to engage in this unpleasant part of your job:

- I don't know what we'll do without you, but we are going to try.
- It's not that you aren't a responsible worker. In fact, you've been responsible for more disasters than any one else in this company.
- I've always told you that it is not a good idea to mix business with pleasure. Today I'm going break that rule. You're fired.
- Tell me—how long have you been with this company, not counting tomorrow?
- I've got good news for you. You won't have to worry about being late for work again.

SMART STEPS

Take complete responsibility. Make a formal announcement that as of a certain date the mantra in your organization will be: *If it's to be, it's up to me.* Consider putting this mantra on business-size cards and distributing them to all employees. Then consistently take complete responsibility for all your actions and insist that everyone else do the same.

Reject the word try. Don't accept the word *try. Try* provides for built-in failure before anyone starts. Even a lack of success will meet the requirements employees have set for themselves. After all, they did try. *Will,* on the other hand, demonstrates commitment, action, and a high probability of success.

Stamp out blame-game conversations. If necessary, make up posters with the words *blame game* crossed out as in European traffic signs. Anytime someone engages in this behavior, point to the poster.

Remind yourself often. Pay attention to what you are recognizing and rewarding. Always keep in mind that over the long term, whatever you reward is what you will get more of, whatever you ignore will go away, and whatever you punish will not be repeated, at least not while you are around.

Foster independent actions. When team members bring you their problems—especially those who complain all the time—ask them to bring you one to three options or solutions for every problem. Then ask them to function as the "primary mover" who puts together a cross-functional team that will address the problem.

Get people to work together. When people are undermining each other, call every one together and ask them what it will take to get them to work together as a team.

Have them put their responses on three by five cards without names.

Continued

Continued

Use each card to drive the discussion.

Then have them make up to five very specific commitments regarding what they will do differently in the future.

Have each one sign the commitment sheet, and then ask them to hold each other accountable. Then catch them doing things right, and let them know about it.

Place people in positions that enable them to build on their strengths. Find out what your team members love to do, and do everything in your power to place them in those positions.

Avoid competition. Have people compete against themselves or against standards. Avoid having people compete against each other within the same organization. The reason: If there is a winner, there will be a loser—and losing demoralizes people, and demoralized people will pull everyone around them down.

Do what's unpopular. Strive to have team members *respect* you, not *like* you. When you want everyone to like you, you'll avoid the tough decisions, you'll avoid confronting the people who need to be confronted, and you'll avoid offering differential rewards based on differential performance because some people might get upset. Ironically, procrastinating on the difficult choices, trying not to get anyone upset at you, and treating everyone equally regardless of their contributions will ensure that the people you'll wind up angering the most are very likely your most productive team members.

As a last resort, resolve conflicts. Serious conflict seldom, if ever, resolves itself. So here is how you can deal with it:

Step 1. When an employee comes to you and complains about another team member, insist that he talk with the other team member in a nonconfrontational manner. If the two can't get things ironed out, ask that *both* come to see you.

Continued

Continued

Step 2. Listen actively to each side of the story. Affirm each person without taking sides. Ask how the conflict is adversely affecting attainment of the mission, vision, and/or core values and strategic goals. Remain objective, and document the facts. Place the focus on work responsibilities. Avoid finding fault or making accusations. Keep attention focused on the present situation, not on past histories or old grievances.

Step 3. Insist on statements of facts rather than opinions. If the employees become emotional, allow them to express their feelings in a nonconfrontational manner and then gently steer the conversation back to the facts.

Step 4. Refer to the company philosophy as behavior guidelines and benchmarks.

Step 5. Judge the issue, not the person; state the desired outcome; and ask each employee for specific suggestions on how the desired outcome can be achieved.

Step 6. Have both parties reach consensus regarding a specific solution. Define the specific outcome and state how it will be measured so that each side will know when it has been achieved. Clearly state who is responsible for what actions within mutually agreed deadline.

Step 7. Write down up to five specific commitments the employees have mutually agreed on, and have them sign the commitment sheet.

When all else fails because the relationship is totally broken, use this approach:

Step 1. Get the two together in a neutral environment, ideally seated at a round table.

Continued

Continued

Step 2. Have each write on a three-by-five card what they like about the other.

Step 3. Have them pass the cards to you. You read them.

Step 4. Have each write a three-by-five card about:

"What I wish were different about you"

"What I wish you would not do"

"What I dislike about you"

Step 5. You read each in turn. At this point it is likely that they will talk freely and you can do away with the cards.

Step 6. Once they talk freely and iron out their differences, have them make up to five specific commitments that define what they will do differently in the future.

Step 7. Write those down on a piece of paper that reads, "We hereby commit to . . . " and have them sign their names before they leave the room.

Prior to concluding the meeting, define your expectation for the future by saying, "I expect that both of you will live by these commitments in the future. I further expect that you will hold each other accountable to these commitments and iron out your differences on your own."

Step 8. Have them agree and shake hands.

15

Don't Worry About Pay

People leave jobs because of dissatisfaction with their boss, lack of challenge, or lack of opportunity for advancement . . . not simply for money.

—Charles O'Reilly

Consider this a week's worth of rewards and recognition, says the boss to her employee as she hands him a weekly paycheck. Even though it is a cartoon, many managers feel that money motivates their employees to deliver peak performance. Nothing could be further from the truth. Want proof? Think about the last time you gave your employees a pay raise. Let's say that it was 5 percent and it became effective the first of the month. How many employees came to work on the first and said, "Boss, today I'll give you 5 percent greater performance." Research tells us that pay will achieve two objectives: It will ensure that employees will come to work, and it will ensure that they stay with your company. This is certainly nothing to complain about, but it is not peak performance. To get that, you have to quit listening to your employees moan and groan about not getting enough money. Think, who has ever come to you and said, "Enough already, you're paying me way to much." (In your dreams, right?) The reality is that money is like love. People seldom, if ever, get enough of it. (I'm assuming here that you have covered the basics and are paying as much or slightly more than the competition. If not, remember another truism: If you pay peanuts, you get monkeys.) No, what you want to do instead is stick to the following 13 rules:

Rule 1. Stimulate Internal Motivation

Want peak performance? Forget money. In fact, forget external rewards—well not quite. (See Rule 13.) There is, however, something far more powerful, far more consistent, and much easier to implement—*internal motivation*. This comes about when employees have something to be passionate about and when you have built a positive organizational culture.

Rule 2. Tie Rewards to Performance

This is the most important management principle of all. I've said it before, and I'll say it again: *What you reward is what you get.* So if you want high performance, then your high performers should be rewarded differently from your low performers. And if you want teamwork, then you must reward . . . (I'm hoping you're getting this). Yet very few managers get this right. One reason: Virtually all employees tend to perceive their performance as "above average." Check this out for yourself. During your next all-hands meeting ask your team members: "How many of you deliver above-average performance?" Watch just about all the hands go up. Now ask: "How many of you deliver average performance?" Virtually none of the hands go up. By the way, I have done this with countless groups, and I have never had anyone raise his hand when I asked who is below average. If you want to figure out how to make this rule work, look at an effective sales organization where people are paid on commission only. Or look at entrepreneurs—such as myself—who only get paid if they produce results.

Rule 3. Tie Rewards to Individual Preferences

Every employee has different wants or, to say it another way, "Different strokes for different folks." For example, if you have a contest and the prize is a trip to Aruba for two, it will not cause someone who is single or afraid to fly to go the extra mile. Similarly, if—as a token of appreciation for a job well done—you provide employees with a ham for the holidays, you likely will achieve the opposite effect for your Jewish employees. (Don't laugh. One of my New York clients did this.) To make this rule come alive, you have to know your employees—what gets them motivated. How do you find that out? You ask them. Now there is a radical concept. If you want to get very efficient, you can collect this information during the employee orientation program—and then keep it updated on an annual basis.

Case in point: REI offers challenge grants to its employees who are virtually all outdoor freaks. Here is how it works: One or several employees come up with an outdoor challenge that they have never done before, such as climbing Mount Everest or biking the new 2600-mile East Coast Greenway that goes from Key West to Calais, Maine. They submit an application describing the outdoor challenge and the gear they need to complete it. Management judges the application and how much of a stretch it is for the employee or group of employees, and if it is approved, REI provides them with free REI equipment to complete the challenge. Instead of worrying about pay, REI gave away $30,000 worth of gear and clothing in 2002. And notice that it caught the attention of the media—read free advertising.[1]

Rule 4. Do It in Public

Whenever possible, recognize team members in front of their colleagues. In fact, here are two practices you *always* should adhere to: Punish in private, and reward in public. You would think that I wouldn't need to talk about something this obvious. Then how come one of my clients used to make it a practice to embarrass his management team members in front of their colleagues? In fact, he said that he practices MBE—are you ready for this—*management by embarrassment*. What were the results? Well, morale was in the toilet. The level of fear was very high. Of course, this MBE leader didn't care about that. His response: "I want them to be fearful. That way they work harder." In fact, the opposite was true. The management team was risk-adverse and very slow to make decisions. Team members wouldn't blow their noses without asking the MBE leader for permission. This was just the opposite of what this team needed, especially since it was operating in a highly competitive global high-tech business.

Instead of practicing MBE, schedule frequent celebrations and hoopla sessions because public recognition is the breakfast of champions. Just think of what Olympic athletes will do to receive a piece of metal on a colorful string around their necks. How about soldiers? They will get themselves shot at for the same piece of worthless metal. Go figure. (And don't write me nasty notes; I'm a retired Lieutenant Colonel, and I've got several pieces of metal on colorful strings.) And please don't tell me that your employees don't like it because they get embarrassed. If this is the case, you have not done a good enough job of building your employees' self-esteem, and it's time to look in the mirror. It likely means that your own level of self-esteem is low. And, of course, you can't give away what you don't have—which you learned about in Chapter 6. If you would like help with this, read—no, wait, devour—my popular book *Make It a Winning Life: Success Strategies for Life, Love and Business.*

Rule 5. Be Fair

Here is a scenario for you to contemplate: Employee number one is a project manager, and completion of one of his projects potentially may save your organization $50,000 over three years. Employee number two has been tinkering with an idea that she came up with on her own time that, on implementation, likely will result in increased sales of about $100,000 indefinitely. How would they feel if they both received a weekend for two at the same resort? The likely perceived inequity could cause employee number two, as well as many others, to conclude that giving 111 percent is not important around here and might provoke her to modify her future actions accordingly. And please don't tell me that you are keeping it secret. That would violate rule 4, and it violates an absolute truism: *There are no secrets in organizations!* Please read that again because there aren't too many absolutes that I know about. More important, I can't even begin to tell you how many leaders all over the world haven't figured this out. They keep spending an inordinate amount of energy trying to keep organizational stuff secret.

Case in point: The other day a senior vice president told her executive team that she was being demoted. Her counterpart from Singapore was going to take her place, and for a period of about one year, she would report to this new executive. She continued, "I wanted you to hear this directly from me instead from the grapevine or the official announcement, which won't be made until about a week from now." She concluded, "This is extremely confidential, and I need to be able to count on you to not have this leave this room." By the following day, the information had gotten all the way to my client's boss in Iceland—that's right. Despite the admonition, one executive had shared the news with his human resources representative, who in turn had e-mailed it to her boss, who was at the time in Iceland. And from there it was just another little e-mail hop to the global boss in Iceland, who was absolutely furious and called my client on the proverbial carpet. Please internalize this truism: *There are absolutely no secrets in organizations.* If you act accordingly, you will have just paid for this book many times over.

Rule 6. Do It in a Timely Manner

If a team member who has gone the extra mile receives a reward or recognition six months later, the reward loses its impact. So do it now. And don't worry if not all employees are present or even if you have to violate rule 4. It's far better to get the recognition one on one than not at all.

A client comes to mind who would on catching employees doing something right randomly take out a crisp new twenty dollar bill and give it to the employee in front of her peers. (Yes, money—if used this way—does result in increased performance. In addition, it has the added advantage of addressing rule 2 because it can be converted into many neat things that employees want.) While doing this, my client always observed rule 7.

Rule 7. Be Specific

When recognizing team members in public, be very clear about what is being rewarded or recognized. As opposed to saying, "I want you all to know that John did a really great job last month," say instead: "Let's all recognize John for helping us live one of our core values, which I know all of you know is to always exceed the customer's expectation. The day before yesterday, Susan Bigshot at the We-Do-It-Right Manufacturing Group urgently needed a set of thingamabobs that we were out of. Instead of telling Susan that he couldn't help her, John called our competitor and had them ship 20 thingamabobs overnight to Susan. Then today David followed up with her to make sure that they met Susan's requirement. That's what I call putting the 'always exceed our customers' expectations' core value to work and is the kind of responsiveness that all of us can be proud of. Let's all give John a big round of applause." This level of specificity allows other team members to emulate the right behavior and increases the probability that similar actions will be repeated.

Rule 8. Do It Randomly

You are violating this rule if employees get upset every time you are *not* rewarding them. Recognizing team members randomly causes the desired behaviors to be more likely repeated and reduces the "what's in it for me" (WIIFM) *entitlement* effect.

I experience this effect in my talks. I like to give out prizes—buttons, audiotapes, CDs, and so on—to people who actively participate. In fact, I throw stuff at people; if nothing else, it keeps them awake. And every time I do it consistently at the beginning of my talk, invariably participants will say: "Hey, where is my prize?" On the other hand, if I space the prizes—give them out randomly—I seldom encounter that question.

Rule 9. Tell Stories

Get extra mileage out of your rewards and recognitions by becoming a storyteller. Telling stories about how Jolly Joe went out of his way to cheer up a depressed patient who was on the verge of taking his life or how Super Sue went the extra mile to ensure that a customer got an order in time to meet a critical deadline helps employees to internalize what's important around here, and begins to shape behavior and performance more effectively than even the best policy you have ever written or the most powerful statistics you have ever presented. For more information, read "Storytelling That Moves People," by Robert McKee, Hollywood's top screenwriting coach.[2]

Rule 10. Recognize Three-Quarters of All Employees

Two common dilemmas leaders face are (1) that those who do not receive a reward get jealous and (2) that the same people get recognized all the time and the others give up. Either way, it means that you are being too stingy. Your goal should be to reward or recognize at least three-quarters of all your employees over the course of a year.(Note: in case you think this is unrealistic, a "thanks for a job well done" handshake counts as recognition.) In this way, *all* team members are more likely to continue to strive for peak performance.

Rule 11. Offer Lots of Variety

Since it is difficult to adhere to rule 3, and since once a reward is received it becomes an expectation, introduce lots of variety all the time. (Bob Nelson's book, *1001 Ways to Reward Employees,* is a great resource.[3]) For example, some of my clients love to recognize extraordinary performance with a 111 percent lapel pin. However, once an employee has received a 111 percent pin, the second one has a much lower perceived value. This is why one of my clients reverted to the old "Green Stamp" approach that allows employees to exchange a specific number of pins for increasingly more valuable prizes.

Rule 12. Get Employees Involved

This rule saves you lots of time and increases your leadership effectiveness dramatically. Get in the habit of always pushing decisions down to the lowest level, especially when you are about to make a decision that has a direct impact on employees' welfare. Ask five volunteers to serve on the rewards and recognition team (please, no more than one manager or supervisor on the team). Give that team a budget, and provide it with the fewest number of rules to make you feel comfortable. Then take your hands off. You will be surprised at the level of creativity and effectiveness. (Use this same approach for most of the decisions you currently make— it works!)

Rule 13. Keep Team Members "Juiced"

Mary Kay sales associates and, for that matter, all highly successful sales professionals have this figured out. You must provide people with external motivation if you want them to consistently perform at peak performance.

(Okay, you caught me. I did tell you under rule 1 that external rewards are not important. Well, they are not *as* important as internal motivation, but they still count.) So, for special occasions—you've achieved the humongous overarching goal (HOG), come in under budget, or had your best year ever—hire a motivational speaker to thank the troops for a job well done. (I happen to know a real good one, wink wink.) If you can't afford that, start building an audio library. Rotate the audio programs to your team members so that they can listen on their way to work. Meet in brief weekly meetings, and have team members share one powerful principle they learned from each audio program. In this way, everyone can learn from everyone else and energize each other at the same time. Or show a motivational videotape during your next training session. Your team members will be positively surprised and at the same time master strategies that will enable them and your company to succeed faster. And oh yes, if you are the skeptic who says, "Well, that stuff doesn't last," then let me remind you that neither does taking a shower, so why do you bother taking one every day?

Follow these 13 rules, and you and your employees will have more fun and get more done, and you'll save money too.

Smile

Employee to boss: "I'm working for a good cause . . . cause I need the money."

SMART STEPS

Have you implemented all the 13 rules discussed in this chapter? If not, why are you looking for more steps?

16

Don't Tell People What to Do

Telling is not leading.
—WOLF J. RINKE

IN SALES THERE IS A WONDERFUL SAYING: Telling is not selling. And so it
is with leading: Telling is not leading. Telling is playing dictator, autocrat,
or boss. (And you know what happened to Hitler, Mussolini, and Saddam
Hussein.) People who are told what to do don't take ownership—and ownership is critical. (How many times have you had your rental car washed
before returning it?) The way you get buy-in is to ask more and assign less,
to involve people, and to listen to people.

Somehow when someone gives us the title of leader many of us think
that we are omnipotent. And with this assumption comes the idea that we
are responsible to tell our people what and how to do it. There is only one
problem with this: You don't know your team members as well as they know
themselves, and you have no clue of what they do. (Stop kidding yourself!)
And since everyone is a composite of strengths and weaknesses, you are not
very likely to help your team members succeed faster by telling them what
to do. The result: Employees become disillusioned and discouraged. In fact,
in a study of 1000 employees, the Gallup Organization of Princeton, New

Jersey, found that 55 percent were not engaged in their jobs and that 19 percent were actively disengaged. These employees ". . . don't know what is expected of them, don't have the materials to do their jobs, and can't get the attention of their bosses." This means that only 26 percent—that's about one in four—of all employees are engaged and are operating at their full potential.[1] (*Wow!* This is a rude wake-up call.) Gallup estimated that disengaged workers cost companies anywhere from $292 billion to $355 billion per year because these workers are less productive, miss more days, and are less loyal.[2] (You'd better read those stats again.)

Worse, some leaders think that they know it all, and this is why they have to tell others what to do. In our culture, making multiple instantaneous decisions with little information is a skill that is admired. We expect dynamic leaders to be able to think on their feet. The bad news is that leaders who use this approach just don't get it. Since they feel that they know it all, they are unable to learn new stuff—this is the readiness-to-learn concept. Uncertainty—which is almost always part of any decision—is just not part of their modus operandi. And so they shoot from the hip instead of being receptive to other people's points of view. The consequences can be devastating. Think of Dennis Kozlowski, CEO of Tyco, who prided himself on being able to make instantaneous decisions, especially when it came to making fast and furious acquisitions. That, in conjunction with suspect accounting practices, caused Tyco to lose about 90 percent of its value in about a year.

In addition, there is another dynamic at play. Like it or not, when you tell people what to do, it causes many people to push back, just to prove to you and maybe to themselves, that no one is going to tell them what to do.

A great way to illustrate this is to have a group of people stand and face each other in dyads. Now ask them to raise their hands about chest high and put their palms against the palms of their partner. Then tell them to push. And invariably you find that the minute you say, "Push," it causes the other partner to push back. The harder the one pushes, the harder the other partner pushes back. Seldom do you find a partner saying to the other, "I'm volunteering not to play this game because it is based on raw power that invariably will have one winner and one loser. And on top of it, both of us likely will be really worn out. Instead, let's find out what we both really want, and then let's put our heads together and figure out what innovative strategies we can come up with that will enable both of us to get what we want."

One of the fastest way improve those statistics is to let people volunteer instead of telling them what to do. When people volunteer, they are more likely to pick the activities, projects, and jobs that they are good at. Voilà—employee satisfaction and productivity go through the roof. And please don't tell me that this does not work. It works at W. L. Gore & Associates, inventor of Gore-Tex fabrics and many other innovative products, and consistently on Fortune's "100 Best Companies to Work For" list. When you show up for work at W. L. Gore you are told: "Find something you love to do." There are no bosses, no one tells associates what to do, and everyone is free to choose to work on any project they wish. By the way, there are also no pay scales. A committee of associates meets every six months to establish pay levels in accordance with associates' contributions.

The Allenberry Story

My first teacher—my father—taught me how to manage. He had a simple management style: "It's my way or it's the highway" or "If I want your opinion, I'll give it to you." This autocratic model stuck with me until many years later. (See Chapter 10 to find out how I cured myself.) At age 21, I was fortunate to land my first management job. It was at Allenberry Resorts in Boiling Springs, Pennsylvania, where I was to be the general manager of the gourmet restaurant—the Carriage Room—and the food and beverage manager for the entire resort. Part of that job involved taking cases of liquor to various functions all over the property with my own car. This is why I was assigned a reserved parking spot right behind the Carriage Room kitchen. I still remember how proud I was. A parking spot with my name on it. Make no mistake, I was hot stuff!

And so it was with a great deal of excitement that I arrived on my first day of work. There was only one problem. Someone was parked in my spot. I walked into the kitchen and in an autocratic manner demanded, "Who is parked in my spot?" Bruno, the chef, told me that he was. But hey, I was his boss, so I told Bruno, "Don't park there anymore. It's my spot. It's got my name on it." Bruno grumbled something under his breath and went about his business. The next day I again arrived at Allenberry with a great deal of anticipation and excitement, just to have it shattered one more time by Bruno. This time I stormed in and said, "Hey Bruno, do

I need to tell you this in German? *Das ist mein Platz und Du darfst da nicht mehr Parken!*" (For those of you who are foreign language–challenged that translates to "That's my parking spot, and I don't want you to park there any more.") Bruno told me that he had been parking in that spot for seven years and that he saw no reason to quit doing so now. Of course, being a great autocratic manager, I told him in no uncertain terms that he was not to park there ever again.

Guess who was parked in my spot when I came to work the next day? That's right, Bruno. And so on the third day I made my father proud: I fired the son-of-a-gun.

Guess what that taught me?

It taught me how to cook, real fast!

Don't Make Decisions

What's the antidote? The first is: Don't make decisions! People are lazy, and that is a good thing. Otherwise, we would still be sitting in a cave and complaining about being cold, tired, and hungry. Virtually all inventions are driven by our need to make our lives simpler, easier, or more pleasant. (Hey, that's why they came up with a remote control.) And because your direct reports are lazy, they will tend to travel the path of least resistance. Instead of thinking, problem solving, or straining their brains—which is tough work—they figure out an easier, more direct route: Ask the boss. Think about it: If you—the leader—make my decisions, you own the "monkey"—that is, you have taken responsibility for *my* work. That makes me ecstatic. Not only is it less work for me, but if your solution bombs, it also will be *your* fault. The outcome: You have just made me dependent on you and made yourself more indispensable. (Of course, this really turns some leaders on because now they can feel really important.) This also means that I will keep coming to you every time I have a problem. Now multiply this by however many direct reports you have, and you know why you work harder than any of your team members and take home the fatter briefcase—better know as a "monkey cage"—than anyone else.

What you want to do instead is to master the art of giving your power away. (A clever consultant came up with a great name—hey, that's what consultants do—*empowering* your team members.) And if you are not giving it away, you are not "growing" people. And if you are not growing people, then what the heck are you doing here anyway? Remember: If in doubt, always push decision making down to the lowest possible level, which you can do by mastering these two powerful phrases:

1. What are *you* going to do about that?
2. What do *you* think?

Lead Like a Coach, Not a Cop

The second antidote is to lead like a coach, not a cop. Unfortunately, many leaders have not mastered this art because they perceive that granting power to their team members will *reduce* their own power. My own experience—as well as that of my clients—has demonstrated just the opposite. Giving power to others not only multiplies your own power, but it also (in the long run) enhances your ability to be a highly contrarian leader (CL).

Before I talk about how to do this, a quick explanation of coaching is in order. *Coaching* is a system that "grows" people by enabling them to learn through guided discovery and hands-on experience. The important element in this definition is that learning occurs through *guided discovery,* not by showing or telling people what to do. Implicit in this definition is that effective coaches have three major responsibilities:

- Guiding people to discover the tools they need to get the job done
- Building confidence
- Helping the "coachee" to be the best he can be

Building confidence and keeping team members motivated are important aspects of leading. Some people will take on additional responsibilities with open arms. No problem there. But what about those who are always running away from additional responsibility? Well, you must make very clear what's in it for them and then reward any degree of success. (Remember: All of us listen to our favorite radio station, WIIFM—*What's in it for me.*) Some employees are afraid of taking on anything new because they are not sure of their own capabilities. Here you must engage them in incremental learning by letting them experience success through the completion of easily attainable "baby steps." In addition, you should point out where and when they have succeeded in the past. Then you must express confidence in their capabilities by saying, for example, "I know you can provide leadership to this team. Remember how well you did last month when you headed up the compensation review project?" In yet other cases you may provide team members with informal or formal training before they are ready to assume the additional responsibility.

How to Coach

Step 1. Agree on the Project or Assignment

This is where you and your "coachee" agree on the specifics of what she is going to be responsible for. These steps, by the way, assume that this project represents an area of strength for you—in other words, you know how to do it in your sleep—and an area of weakness for your coachee—something that would enhance her competence and, once mastered, would take a load off your shoulders. Of course, many leaders hesitate to provide this type of coaching because, according to them, they lack the time. Deep down they are really afraid that they will coach themselves right out of a job. (How do you feel about that?) Nothing, of course, could be further from the truth.

Step 2. Mutually Identify the Goals and Outcomes Expected

I call this *defining a good job*. So often things don't go the way you expect because your coachee didn't really understand the outcomes you wanted to achieve in the first place. When you are done with this step, both of you should be very clear about the when, where, what, who, and how. Let me emphasize that you always should set high expectations because that will help determine how successful your team members will become. The reason is that in the long run *you get the type and quality of performance you expect, measure, and accept.* (Darn, this stuff is complicated, isn't it?) This is especially true because research tells us that approximately three out of four employees are performing well below their maximum potential.

Step 3. Facilitate Self-Discovery

This is the step that distinguishes coaching from delegating. It is probably the most difficult step for most leaders, especially those who are used to telling others what to do.

To make this happen:

- Listen actively—listen for the meaning, not just the words. This requires you to make your own mind quiet and talk less—a lot less. Remember, there must be a reason that *you were born with two ears and only one mouth.* Maybe you were meant to listen twice as much as you talk, especially when coaching others.
- Help your coachees think through the process and consequences of their proposed actions. This means that *they* do the thinking. To ensure that this happens, you might ask, "What would be the consequences of you taking this action?" Remember, your role is to facilitate their thought processes, *not* to think for them.
- Share your good and *bad* experiences. Your coachees will learn from both. Most leaders hesitate to share how they have messed up. They feel that they must maintain a facade of perfection. However, sharing what has *not* worked for you, especially your really bad goofs, is particularly helpful. It makes you more human, gets you off the pedestal, and gives your coachees permission to be less than perfect—which is what we all are anyway.

Step 4. Agree on the Boundaries

If you have identified and implemented a widely shared organizational philosophy—your mission, vision, and core values—most of step 4 is already done. (If you don't know what I'm talking about, reread Chapter 11.) After all, your philosophy represents the mutually accepted parameters and boundaries in your organization. They are the "gold standard" for everyone on your team. Of course, you may need to verbally supplement them so that your coachees know where your comfort zone is and where the danger zone begins. You also may want to define when you want to be briefed and what type of feedback you want, for example, whether you want it in writing or in person.

Step 5. Authorize and Empower

To get the job done, team members must have the authority to take independent actions. I refer to this as "giving your team members rope." This includes the appropriate spending authority to get the job done. And please don't be timid here. After all, if *employees* at Ritz Carlton hotels have the ability to spend up to $2000 to solve customer service problems, what's your excuse?[3] To make this work, you also must master the art of letting go. I mean really letting go and giving away your power. You see, it is virtually impossible to learn by doing if your team members have to check with you every time they need to make a decision or a change. They would spend all their time running after you instead of taking care of business. In other words, you must tell your team members how far they can go without coming to you, and then you must stay out of their way and let them do their thing. This has been particularly hard for leaders who are afflicted with that dreaded "perfectionitis" disease. (I used to suffer from that.) When they see something wrong, they instinctively want to correct it right away. The better way is to let team members learn from their own mistakes. "But," you protest, "let them make a mistake and not say *anything?*" Yes, that's what I mean. "All the time, regardless of the consequences?" No, that's why being a highly effective contrarian leader is an art first and a science second. You must do a risk-benefit analysis. This is what physicians are taught to do anytime they prescribe medication. They weigh the benefits of the medication against the risks associated with it. You must do the same thing when making a decision about how much rope you should give your team members.

Step 6. Summarize and Reality Test

The purpose of this step is to enhance communication accuracy. If the project is critical, do some reality testing by having the coachee state in her own words what, specifically, the two of you have agreed to. A good way to accomplish this is to say, "As you well know, Jane, this is a critical project for us. Please be kind enough to summarize for me what it is that you are going to do between now and the next time we meet." Assuming that at this point you are both singing from the same sheet of music, you'll be ready to move to the next step.

Step 7. Track and Follow Through

This step is designed to make sure that nothing falls between the cracks. It is especially critical if you are coaching someone for the first time. In such a case, you will want to be sure to put a note on your calendar or your personal digital assistant (PDA) that will remind you of the date and time your coachee promised to provide you with an update or any other kind of feedback. Once this is achieved, stand back—yes, really stand back—and whatever you do, don't—let me say it again, *don't*—interfere. Now watch your team members grow, and watch the dramatic improvements in performance and productivity.

Step 8. Celebrate, Reward, and Recognize

Your coachee has done a great job, and so you do what lots of managers do, *punish* her. Hey, don't get mad at me, at least give me a minute and let me explain. Most managers—okay, not you; after all, you are a contrarian leader—know who the "water walkers" are on their team. And they are the folks who get even more projects piled on top of their daily responsibilities. This is called *punishment* unless something positive happens to these water walkers that does not happen to anyone else. Hence it's critical that you don't forget step 8—celebrate, reward, and recognize. Recognize a job well done, and make that celebration commensurate with the size of the job. Big job, *big* celebration, reward, or recognition—I know you're catching on. And be sure to do it publicly whenever you can. (If this does not sound familiar, reread Chapter 15.)

Smile

Excerpt from a new employee manual:

Personal Days

Each employee will receive 104 personal days a year. They are called Saturday and Sunday.

SMART STEPS

Anytime you assign a project to a team or a team member, explain the *why* and let him figure out the *how*. And then get out of his way.

Give your team members more power than you think is wise because the more of your responsibilities you give away—delegate—the more powerful and effective you become. Moreover, this is really the only way that you will be able to "grow" people. And the more your team members grow, the more—you guessed it—you grow.

Involve people, especially in decisions that have a direct impact on them, such as parking spaces, training opportunities, work schedules, and believe it or not, even pay.

Reduce the number of rules and standard operating procedures (SOPs) by 50 percent this month. Continue cutting them by 50 percent until you are down to the absolute minimum. Not in charge? Then start lobbying the powers that be now. Nothing suffocates and demotivates team members more than stuff that gets in the way of their being able to do a great job. And this is what most rules and SOPs do.

If a team member comes to you and asks you to make a decision, ask her, "What do you think?" Then let her go with that decision unless it will inflict harm to customers, is contraindicated by the organizational philosophy, or costs more than you can safely sustain.

17

Don't Satisfy Customers

Service is just a day-in, day-out, ongoing, never-ending, unremitting, persevering, compassionate type of activity.

—LEON GORMAN, OF L.L. BEAN

WAIT, YOU SAY, I THOUGHT CUSTOMER SATISFACTION is the key to business success. Yes, it's the ticket to get into the ball game, but it won't ensure that you are going to win! To demonstrate, I ask my seminar audiences to think of a recent service encounter that they remember. (What do you remember?) People consistently recall the extremes—service providers who *messed up* and those who *exceeded* their expectations. Seldom does anyone recall a service provider who has *met* their expectation, that is, satisfied them. This means that only if you and your team members consistently *exceed* your customers' expectations will customers remember you and your organization. Otherwise, you will be off their radar screens. And if they forget you, they will not think of you the next time they, a friend, a family member, or an acquaintance needs the type of service you offer. And if they forget you and your organization often enough, you'll feel the impact on your bottom line real soon.

How much of an impact? According to researchers who analyzed the buying behaviors of 1500 PNC Bank customers, there was clear evidence that customers who ranked themselves as "highly satisfied" (the highest level of satisfaction) maintained a bank balance of nearly 20 percent greater than customers who were "satisfied" (the second highest level of satisfaction).[1] Wouldn't you love your customers to purchase your products or services 20 percent more often than they currently do?

The researchers also compared the impact of different levels of satisfaction on profitability by dividing 400 PNC branches into three tiers. The top tier contained the 15 percent of the branches that had the highest percentage of highly satisfied customers. The middle tier consisted of the middle 70 percent, and the bottom tier consisted of the 15 percent of the branches that had the fewest highly satisfied customers. Using revenue per employee—a key indicator of bank profitability—researchers found that the top-tier branches had 23 percent higher than average revenue, whereas the middle tier fell 3 percent and the bottom tier fell 9 percent below average revenue. Could you do with 23 percent higher revenue?

The researchers concluded: "Those [customers] displaying the highest level of satisfaction are, in economic terms, significantly more attractive than those showing only moderate levels of satisfaction. And a customer who stays highly satisfied becomes steadily more attractive over time."[2]

AquaGuard Gets Customers to Say "Wow!"

Of course, the question is how do you exceed customers' expectations? You do it by getting every customer to say "Wow!" One way is to take a look at what your competition is doing and to do something *different*. (This is what this whole book is about.) Case in point is AquaGuard, a Beltsville, Maryland, waterproofing company that has achieved exceptional growth by being a very aggressive service provider in an industry that has a very poor customer service track record. The company's mission, which is known by every team member, drives AquaGuard's strategy: "To achieve unrivaled customer satisfaction and 'peace of mind' by providing the highest quality, most innovative waterproofing services." The way the company executes this mission is to start every customer interface on a positive note by avoiding high-pressure sales tactics. In fact, prospective customers are urged *not* to schedule an appointment with a technician until *after* they have talked to several AquaGuard customers. This is the first "Wow!" Technicians who call on customers serve in a consultative capacity to help solve the customer's problem, *not* to make a sale. And if attaching downspouts that came off during the last storm can solve the problem, this is what the technician will do—at *no charge*. This is the second "Wow!" If, on the other hand, the customer requires waterproofing, an estimate will be provided that typically will be *more costly* than that of the company's competitors.

Several days after friendly, highly skilled technicians who have been trained in customer service complete the work, an AquaGuard representative calls the customer to make sure that the work was completed to the customer's utmost satisfaction. (At that time, the rep also asks several other questions to track the effectiveness of the company's customer service strategy and to tie employee rewards to performance.) This is the third "Wow!" If the customer is not delighted, AquaGuard will cheerfully—and I do mean cheerfully—fix the problem to the customer's total satisfaction. This is the fourth "Wow!" It shouldn't be, but it is, especially in the waterproofing business—which most customers perceive to be to the extreme left of the stereotypical used car salesperson. The customer will receive another call after the first big rain storm to ascertain if the waterproofed area stayed dry. Now that's a can't-believe, knock-your-socks-off quadruple "Wow!" Customers are so blown away by this call that they can't wait to tell their neighbors, friends, and relatives. This is exactly AquaGuard's long-term strategy because the company's vision, which is known by every team member, is "To consistently exceed our customers' expectations and become the standard by which all waterproofing companies are measured." In short, for AquaGuard it is far more important to generate positive word-of-mouth referrals, the most powerful and effective advertising strategy at the disposal of any business, than to make a sale.

Has it had a positive impact on the bottom line? Well, I'll let you be the judge. Even though AquaGuard shut down its telemarketing department in 1997—it was not in keeping with the company's mission, vision, and core values—the company generated 62.5 percent *more* sales in 2002 compared with 1998 with 20 percent *fewer* employees and a 75 percent reduction in advertising expenses and an overall cost savings of 42 percent compared with 1998. At the same time, the company's referral rate has increased by 305 percent per year, and overall profits have increased—are you ready for this?—240 percent. This is what I call "Wow!" results.

If you like these results, get started now! Develop a service-driven philosophy, define your expectations to every team member (get every customer to say "Wow!"), provide team members with intensive training, empower them to do whatever it takes to *exceed* every customer's expectation, aggressively measure service satisfaction, and tie employee rewards to service improvements. Will this help you grow *your* business? Absolutely! After all, there are many service providers that satisfy their customers, but there are very few that consistently *get their customers to say* "*Wow!*"

Pizza in the Sky: How to Benefit from Service *Failures*

I couldn't believe it! I was being put on my flight back home to Washington/Dulles early. But wait, I'm getting ahead of myself. I had had a demanding but gratifying day that started with a wake-up call at 5:30 A.M. I delivered a motivational opening session for the largest manufacturer of canned vegetables in the world in Rochester, New York, followed by an intensive sales seminar after lunch. And the day went wonderfully. With only a small degree of modesty, I am proud to tell you that for both programs I received a standing ovation. But then I was absolutely stunned when I arrived at the Rochester airport about 30 minutes early and was told by the United Express agent, "Dr. Rinke, we can put you on a flight right now. It will get you to Washington/Dulles 30 minutes early." This was music to my ears, especially since I had been on the road for several days and could hardly wait to sleep in my own bed.

So I grabbed my McDonald's bag and jumped aboard. Just before UA 7578 was ready to take off, the door was reopened, and the gate agent told us, "Ladies and gentlemen, I have bad news for you. We've just been locked out from Dulles, and I need to ask you to get off the plane and go back into the terminal until at least 6:00 P.M., at which time we will receive an update regarding the status at Washington/Dulles."

Off the plane we went. No big deal. After all, it gave me an opportunity to eat my now-cold McDonald's "unhappy" meal in the terminal instead of on a shaky little puddle jumper. However, several of the other passengers were a bit more distraught. The reason: Flight UA 7578 had a *scheduled* departure time of 3:30 P.M.

At about 6:00 P.M. we were told that our new departure time was now 6:50 P.M. Shortly before that time, everyone was asked to get back on board for an "immediate departure." You guessed it. Immediate was not so immediate because once 7:00 P.M. rolled around the pilot advised us that we had to wait once again a "bit longer." Apparently, continued thunderstorms were delaying all flights into Washington/Dulles, so we sat and waited some more. No problem for me. It gave me a chance to catch up on work. However, other passengers, especially those with connecting flights, were more upset. Finally, at about 7:25 P.M. we were given the go-ahead to make our short 65-minute flight from Rochester to Washington/Dulles.

After we had been in the air for about 90 minutes, the pilot advised us that we had been placed in a holding pattern due to turbulent weather at Washington/Dulles. What was unusual was that the pilot was very empathetic and "told us more than we wanted to know." He truly seemed sorry that this was such a fiasco. Also unusual was the young flight attendant—Amy—who was extremely cheerful and helpful. (What a concept!) Being responsive to every passenger who had a question, she was able to defuse a lot of apprehension and somehow made the flight not nearly as bad as it really was. She even began to serve free beer and wine. After circling the not-so-friendly-sky for about two and a half hours, the pilot told us that he was getting low on fuel and that we needed to land in Charlottesville, Virginia, to refuel. By the time we landed, it was about 10:30 P.M. Once again, we were asked to get off the plane so that we could be more comfortable. This sounded better than being stuck in a holding pattern in a puddle-jumper, except that the little Charlottesville airport had been virtually closed for the night. We were confined to the boarding area, and the only thing that was open was the restrooms. (Why do they call them restrooms—have you ever rested in one?) After about a 50-minute wait, we were asked to reboard, and the pilot told us that he had been given a slot and that we had better hustle so that we could make it. No sooner had everyone fastened their seat belts when the pilot told us that we regrettably had lost our slot once again. And would we please get off the plane again. By then it was just about midnight, and several passengers, such as one mom with her six-year-old son, had been traveling for 18 hours.

On exiting the plane the pilot talked briefly with every passenger and assured us that the crew wanted to get home just as much as we did. However, since he could not give us a specific "wheels up" time, he would be happy to put anyone up in a hotel. Everyone, except the mom with the six-year-old boy, camped out in the waiting area hoping for a miracle. And the miracle came in the form of Amy, who cheerfully announced that she had ordered pizza and soft drinks for everyone. I was amazed how much that seemed to cheer everyone up. Just as the pizza arrived some 35 minutes later, Amy let us know that we had been given the go-ahead. So Amy grabbed all the pizza boxes and soft drinks and told us, "No problem, I'll get this served in route." After we finally had taken off, Amy served us our preference of pizza. Despite the late hour, Amy continued to be very pleasant and cheerful. Actually, it felt more like we were at a ball game than in the air. Amy maintained that level of positive energy even after she dropped an entire pizza on the floor, barely missing a passenger (me). She was even able to provide us with seconds and got all that done in the 14-minute flight. When we finally landed at Washington/Dulles shortly after 1:00 A.M., everyone thanked the crew for a *job well done*. Mind you, for most passengers, the approximately one-hour flight took nine and a half hours. And still they thanked the crew for "doing a great job."

What are the lessons that you can learn form this? Don't worry about service failures. They will happen in any business. It's not the failure that will cause you to lose customers. It's how frontline service providers respond that will make or break your business. After all, research tells us that unsatisfied customers are very talkative. They have a habit of telling everybody—more correctly, about 21 others—about an unsatisfactory service experience. Unfortunately, this is a very costly proposition because it literally destroys positive word of mouth, the only advertising that really works. It is also extremely costly because it will cost you roughly five times as much to attract a new customer compared with retaining a current customer. In addition, research tells us that you can increase profits by 25 to 85 percent merely by retaining 5 percent more of your current customers.[3]

Smile

It was mealtime, and the flight attendant asked the passenger if he would like dinner. "What are my choices?" the customer asked. "Yes or No," replied the flight attendant.

SMART STEPS

Hire only people who have a service personality. That is, hire people who are positive, enthusiastic, empathetic, resilient, resourceful, enterprising, and creative.

Treat all employees as if they are winners, adults, and team members. At the Ritz Carlton, employees are told, "We are all ladies and gentlemen, serving ladies and gentlemen." Never forget that over the long run you get what you expect.

Provide every new team member with a comprehensive and fun orientation program. Let's face it, you can't expect your team members to deliver consistently excellent service if you treat them like mushrooms.

Provide meaningful and ongoing job-related continuing education and training. If you don't, your excellent employees will leave you because they know that unless they are learning and growing, they are falling behind, and if they do that long enough, they will become an "endangered species."

Celebrate longevity. You can't continue to sustain high levels of employee turnover. (For the real cost associated with turnover see Chapter 10.)

Adhere to an aggressive internal promotion policy. Help your team members to succeed and grow, and they will more likely stick with you for the long term.

Collect and publicly display detailed customer satisfaction data. Do this in a manner that is understood by all team members. Use graphs and charts whenever you can. Everyone understands pictures better than numbers.

Tie rewards to performance. Reward customer service champions differently than your average service provider.

Continued

Continued

Publicly celebrate customer service heroes. When you celebrate, be sure to tell stories about the specifics of team members exceeding customers' expectations. It lets team members know what's important around here.

Use your abundant mental energy to catch your team members doing things right. This builds service providers' level of self-esteem. And only team members who feel good about themselves, their organization, and their boss will be able to exceed customers' expectations consistently.

Make taking care of customers fun! Remember: If it's fun, it gets done!

Don't Downsize

You can't downsize yourself to profitability.
—Wolf J. Rinke

The verdict is in: Downsizing does not work if you use *long-term* profitability as the measure of success—at least not in about 70 percent of the cases. Why? Because you gain the competitive advantage *through* people, *not* by getting rid of them. So why are executives literally overdosing on downsizing, rightsizing, or is it capsizing? For example, according to U.S. Department of Labor, Bureau of Labor Statistics, Mass Layoff Statistics, throughout 2002, large and midsize businesses laid off about 2 million workers. This is an average of 100 workers in approximately 20,000 separate events. (That's a lot of downsizing.) And looking at the current unemployment statistics things are continuing to get worse. So why does this downsizing trend continue? Here are my top three reasons. Number one: It's the in thing to do—hey, everyone else is doing it, so it must be working. Number two: It does make the balance sheet look better, often much better over the *short term*—the emphasis is on the words *short term*. And number three: It is extremely lucrative for executives and consultants. Executive compensation is often tied to corporate financial performance, and of course, many consultants specialize in downsizing. (By the way, I'm assuming that you have an effective performance management system in place that weeds out below average or C players on a regular basis. To me, this is not downsizing; it's simply good human resources management.)

It's unreasonable to expect employees to sustain high productivity if they have been asked to work themselves out of a job. Worse, most companies buy high and sell low. They lay off during times when demand for their products is low. This is usually the time when employees are plentiful, that is, less expensive. Then they go on a hiring spree when demand is high, that is, when employees are scarce and more expensive. Since, on average, it costs between one and one and a half years' salary to replace a typical employee, it becomes rather obvious that you want to use downtimes to educate, train, and develop your most valuable team members, not lay them off, so that when demand increases, as it usually does, your company will be ready to take advantage of it. But, you protest, my business is slowing down; my profits are dwindling; the only thing I can do is massive layoffs. *Wrong!* In fact, firing may be exactly the opposite of what you want to do. Here is why:

Have you ever observed the behavior of your employees during a snowstorm? They are listening to the radio, watching the Weather Channel, and constantly looking out the window and calling their loved ones to find out how the roads are. In short, they are focusing on everything except their work. Similar behavior occurs during massive layoffs. Employees crank up the grapevine, spend too much time at the proverbial water cooler, and send incessant e-mails to find out who got canned. In addition, everyone becomes extremely riskadverse, only doing the things they know will be safe. In addition, it's likely that your best employees have polished their résumés and are beginning to shop around. As a result, your organizational climate turns negative, further diminishing your productivity and profitability. This is exactly the opposite behavior you want when your business is heading south. Here is a better way:

Seven Ways to Improve Profitability without Downsizing

1. Let Employees Cut the Fat

I see it all the time. In fact, just two weeks ago one of my coaching clients, Jon, the vice president of information technology (IT) at a high-tech company in charge of 450 employees was told to cut 70 full-time equivalents

(FTEs). When I asked Jon if he had the option to come up with comparable cost savings elsewhere, he said that he was told *no* by senior management. I just don't get it? Why are most executives missing the unequivocally most powerful strategy to maintain morale, increase performance and productivity, and reduce costs all at the same time? How do you do that? It's simple, Watson, you *involve* team members.

There is simply no better or faster way to improve the profitability of your company than by cutting costs. This is why most managers immediately think of downsizing when their business is going poorly. After all, for most companies, labor is the biggest expense. However, you can't downsize yourself to profitability. What you want to do instead is to involve your employees. Announce the severity of the challenges the company is facing. Share with your employees that layoffs are an absolutely last resort and that your preference is to take advantage of your team members' creativity to bring costs in line. One of the best ways to do this is to form "Expense Buster Teams" in each business unit, department, or organization. Establish cost-cutting goals for each team. Tell them that nothing is sacred, provided that it does not interfere with accomplishment of the company's mission, vision, and core values and attainment of the humongous overarching goal (HOG). Acknowledge submitted suggestions within 24 hours, and have them reviewed and implemented as soon as possible. Add to the excitement by conducting an "Expense Buster Contest" with prizes for the best cost-cutting ideas. Make everything public, celebrate functional ideas in a big way, and watch your expenses shrink beyond your wildest dreams.

2. Be Visible

Visibility and accessibility help to shrink the grapevine and ensure that your employees are working more and worrying less during uncertain times. In addition, think about it, you're not finding solutions to your problems when you are practicing management by sitting in the office (MBSITO). To do that, you have to spend at least 66 percent of your time with the people who can help you solve your problems—your employees and your customers. Therefore, this is a great time to develop a powerful habit—the habit of practicing management by walking around (MBWA). Get started right now by blocking time out every week on your calendar for MBWA. (And for the skeptics, research has clearly demonstrated that leaders who focus on their people, instead of the work, are *more* productive.[1])

3. Contact Defectors

This is a great time to have your employees check with your customers, especially the ones you value the most—your high-volume customers—to find out how you can continue to exceed their expectations (see Chapter 17). And since business is down, this means that employees are not very busy, so put them to work contacting defectors—customers who have not done business with your company for the past year. Have your team members ask defectors what it will take to have them do business with you again. Then act on it, and watch your business grow to unexpected new heights.

4. Improve Training

Yes, you read correctly, do *more* training. I'm painfully aware that education, training, and development are virtually almost always the first things that bite the dust when the going gets tough. However, think about it. This slowdown, like every slump that preceded it, will turn around, and when it does, you want your people to be ready to take advantage of the next boom. Besides, this is the best time to do more retraining and cross-training because your people have the time for it. If you are like most companies I consult with, you are not doing enough training anyway. According to the American Society for Training and Development, training expenditures across all industries in the United States for 2001 were only $761 per training-eligible employee, which translates to 1.9 percent of payroll or an average of 23.7 hours of training per year.[2]

Actually, there is *not* a lot of magic here, proving again that the problem with common sense is that it is not very common: If you want your organization to get better, your people have to get better. Think about it. With competition getting fiercer every day, educating, training, and developing your team members will be cost-effective over the long run and assure your organization a more loyal workforce that has bought into your organizational culture and philosophy.

5. Practice MBA

You need a powerful strategy to combat *negativities* so prevalent during tough times. The best way to do this is to practice management by appreciation (MBA) as opposed to management by exception (MBE). To get started, focus your energy on catching people doing things almost *right*, and then let them know about it, publicly, if at all possible. (If you need more help, read my book *Winning Management: 6 Fail-Safe Strategies for Building High-Performance Organizations.*[3])

6. Grow People

If you want to increase your power, you must master the art of giving it away. And if you are not giving it away, you are not "growing" people. To do this, you have to ask yourself, "Am I behaving more like a coach or a cop," and then modify your behavior accordingly. Also make it a practice to always push decision making down to the lowest possible level. This is the best time for team members to learn new skills and become more effective decision makers. So coach them to make that happen (for specifics, see Chapter 16).

7. Lead by Example

If you must downsize, be sure to lead by example by having the entire executive team take a dramatic *real* pay cut commensurate with the level of downsizing. There is nothing more hypocritical than firing a certain percentage of employees across the board without making any sacrifices at the executive level. It's simply obscene, especially since U.S. executives are making an average of 411 times what frontline employees are making—this is up from 85 times in 1990, all while business results—regardless of how measured—have continued to decrease.[4] For example, in 2002, median compensation for chief executive officers (CEOs) was $13.2 million, *up* by 14 percent from 2001, even though the Standard & Poor's 500 Index was *down* by 22.1 percent.[5] Instead of tying pay to performance, CEOs have been able to tie pay to *non*performance. In fact, *Fortune* magazine concluded that about the only thing CEO pay is tied to is "how much the people in their compensation committee make in their day jobs—often as CEOs at other companies."[6]

Before you go to an overall reduction in force (RIF), take advantage of voluntary systems such as attrition and early retirement. If those don't result in enough savings, experiment with other creative initiatives, such as hiring freezes, salary freezes or cuts, shortened workweeks, restricted overtime hours, unpaid vacations, temporary plant or office closures, or any of the strategies that follow.

Five Ways to Downsize "Lite"

1. Transfer Jobs

You may be able to retain employees by allowing them to transfer to other jobs, departments, or facilities. Be sure to announce such transfer opportunities in advance of the downsizing so that employees know that they may be able to avoid layoffs by changing jobs or work sites.

2. Establish Alliances

If downsizing is still necessary, establish partnerships with other organizations. For example, when Emery Worldwide Airlines needed to eliminate several thousand employees nationwide, it partnered with the U.S. Postal Service, which hired many of the downsized Emery employees. Everybody won. Emery was able to achieve its reduction in force (RIF) without incurring outplacement and unemployment expenses; employees continued to be employed, many in similar positions; and the Postal Service gained trained employees.

3. Cut Pay Across the Board

Instead of reducing your workforce by a certain percentage across the board, cut pay and work hours for the entire workforce to achieve the needed reductions in costs. This is an option that many employees prefer. For example, employees at a unionized Saturn plant voted to work four hours less each week to avoid an organization-wide downsizing. This provided a triple win for all concerned. In addition, after business picked back up, the trained employees resumed their previous 40-hour work schedule. By the way, keep this equitable by making the cuts across the board, not like US Airways CEO David Siegel, who exacted steep pay and benefit cuts from airline employees while he received about $1.45 million in salary and bonuses, almost double the compensation that his predecessor was paid the previous year.[7]

4. Encourage Phased Retirement

Instead of full-fledged retirement, encourage employees to accept a phased retirement, providing employees the opportunity to scale down their work hours and income on a gradual basis over a specified period of time. Losing your most experienced employees can have numerous unintended consequences. For example, when the District of Columbia (DC) government downsized about 3000 employees, it lost over 60,000 years of experience, including a computer information services manager who was responsible for performing virus inspections. The result was a massive system-wide crash that cost the DC government dearly. Offering employees a phased-down retirement opportunity provides the organization access to the employees' knowledge, reduces labor costs, and keeps employees loyal and employed.

5. Provide for Early Retirement and Voluntary Severance

The upside of this is that early-retirement programs will tend to encourage the departure of relatively highly paid employees. The downside is that you tend to lose your most experienced team members. However, it is still preferable to an across-the-board RIF.

If you still need to do more, trim very selectively, focusing primarily on employees who add the least value while minimizing the negative impact on the remaining organization. And after you have achieved the needed reductions in labor costs, get busy overcommunicating with the survivors to give them a sense of assurance and safety. Also find out what additional training and development they will need so that they can pick up the pieces from the departed team members and maintain productivity. Then begin the strategic process of changing your human resources paradigm by implementing the following strategies, which are designed to prevent future RIFs.

Four Ways to Avoid Future Cuts

1. Implement an Effective Performance Management System

Your employees are assets to be deployed, not costs to be cut. This is why you need to evaluate your business plan and your employees' performance on a regular basis to make sure that people and organizational requirements are aligned and that all employees are adding value. At least twice a year you need to identify your A, B, and C players, so that you can provide A team members—these are your "water walkers"—with increasingly challenging assignments and B players—average performers—with continuing education, training, and development to help them be the best they can be. Your C players—marginal and poor performers—who add little value and are not interested or able to move themselves into the B category need to be asked to leave. (Both you and the employee ultimately will be much happier and more productive. See my article, "Getting Fired Is the Best Thing That Can Happen to You."[8]) If you manage your people aggressively in this way, you will reduce dramatically the need for future downsizing.

2. Install a Performance-Based Compensation System

A well-designed performance-based compensation system with a relatively small base salary and generous performance incentives that are tied to individual, team, and organizational performance will align your labor costs with organizational performance and reduce the need for RIFs. An example of such a system is one developed by the steel manufacturer Nucor Corporation, where frontline employees work in self-directed teams of 20 to 40 people and are compensated as follows:

- Hourly base pay is 25 to 33 percent below the industry average.
- A bonus of 80 to 200 percent of base pay is paid weekly to all *teams* that meet or exceed productivity goals. Productivity rankings are posted daily.
- Employees who are five minutes late lose their bonus for the day. Those who are 30 minutes late lose their bonus for the week.
- Products returned for poor quality result in a proportionate decrease in bonus pay.

As a result, Nucor is more than twice as productive as its competitors. Specifically, Nucor produces a ton of steel in 45 minutes versus three hours for the big steel makers. Nucor's employees are paid 60 percent more than other employees in the industry.[9]

3. Install an Entrepreneurial Culture

In this era of intensifying global competition, this strategy is an absolute must. It is simply no longer reasonable to give your employees the impression that they have permanent job security. By the same token, it is equally unreasonable for you to expect long-term loyalty from your team members. Instead, an entrepreneurial culture maintains that we form a partnership where the employer provides the employee with an opportunity to apply his skills, talents, and abilities, for which he is compensated, provided that he achieves specific goals that add value and contribute to the bottom line. To make sure that the partnership continues to be mutually beneficial, you—the leader—provide your team members with lots of opportunities for growth and achievement, which, in turn, improves their productivity and their ability to market themselves successfully to other organizations. This causes your team members to stick around. The partnership ceases to exist when it is no longer rewarding or profitable for either party, at which time the "entrepreneur" moves on.

4. Make Greater Use of Just-in-Time Employees

The increasingly cruel competitive landscape will require you to make greater use of consultants, independent contractors, temporary employees, and outsourcing—a just-in-time workforce that can expand or contract more easily to meet your current needs. For example, of the 900 employees at the Hutchinson Technology plant, makers of disk drive components in Eau Claire, Wisconsin, a full 20 percent are part-time and temp workers. In addition, when demand for the company's products increases—which doesn't happen very often—full-time employees are asked to work overtime, which allows the company to flex up so that it can stay competitive.[10]

Smile

Government studies show that a 7 percent unemployment level is acceptable to 93 percent of the working population.

SMART STEPS

This chapter is chock-full of smart steps. Go get busy and apply them.

19

Don't Respond to the Urgent

Time is a rubber band. You will get everything done that has to get done, no matter how little or how much time you have.

—WOLF J. RINKE

THE PRODUCTIVITY OF MOST MANAGERS STINKS. Why? Because they pay too much attention to the urgent. Putting out fires may be a key skill for firefighters, but it will keep you in the minor leagues as a leader. I'm currently in the process of coaching nine senior managers from a global company. And the one thing that all of them have in common is that they are totally overwhelmed. And this is so despite the fact that they typically work 10- to 12-hour days, being connected 24/7 to their electrical umbilical cord—better known as a Blackberry, a personal digital assistant (PDA)–cell phone combination that is always on—and rarely, if ever, take a vacation. So what is the problem?

One of the biggest problems is that they are always connected and that each e-mail and phone call becomes an urgent issue that must be responded to immediately. And the urgent calls just keep on coming, one seemingly more important than the other. And before you know it, another day has passed without any concentrated think time and without any time to attack major projects that have an impact on the bottom line.

In short, they have very little control over their second most precious resource—the only resource that cannot be bought, borrowed, rented, hired, or produced. Unlike people, we can't hire more; unlike equipment, we can't upgrade it, and finally, unlike money, which most of us worry a great deal about, we cannot make any more of it. It is precious because it is the only commodity that is required for everything we do, and it is totally perishable and absolutely irreplaceable. In fact, the only thing that is more precious is our health. What is this sterling commodity? It is *time*.

So let's take a look what you can do to manage your time more effectively. Come to think of it, *time management* is a misnomer. Each of us is provided with 24 hours every day. No matter how well you manage it, it still only adds up to 24 hours. Instead of managing time, we manage and prioritize the activities in those 24 hours. And we get everything done that we perceive to be important. (Read that again; it is a critical concept.) Before you nix this idea, please pause a moment, reflect, and recall the one thing that is *the* most important activity in your personal or professional life. On the personal side, it may be being with your family, football, or gardening. On the professional side, it may be making more money, being recognized by your peers, or getting promoted. Now think back: How often are you not able to devote enough time to whatever it is that is *the* most important thing to you? I bet that it doesn't happen very often, does it? In other words, most people *make* time to do all the things they consider important. I call this approach to time management the *rubber band approach*.[1]

Here is what you can do to stretch the time rubber band without breaking it.

Chunk Your Time

I'm sure that your work is characterized by constant interruptions from phone calls, beepers, voice mail, e-mail, employees, and coworkers. For most of us, uninterrupted time is almost nonexistent. We go from one urgent requirement to another. Instead of having time to do the important stuff, such as developing and coaching team members or coming up with a new strategy to better serve our customers, most of us are busy putting out one fire after another. However, if you are to make sound decisions and solve important long-range problems, you must have a big chunk of time. And the first step in that process is to "routinize" crisis.

"Routinize" Crisis

You must learn to manage crises—the urgent—instead of the crisis managing you. That is accomplished by first putting out the fire and then going one step further and analyzing the crisis. Ask: What is the pattern here? Why did it occur? What can we do to avoid it in the future? and Who can be trained to prevent this occurrence in the first place? Then implement actions designed to prevent it from happening again. Now I can just hear you saying that you are too busy putting out fires; you don't have time for extensive, time-consuming analyses. In other words, you are in a time trap. To get out of this trap, you must begin to analyze how you spend your time, get rid of your time wasters, and learn how to chunk your time. So let's begin by looking at your current time utilization.

Establish Critical Priorities

The reason why the urgent requirements are messing up your day is that everything that presents itself becomes urgent. And the only way to deal with this is to get very clear about your top three priorities—I call these the *winning-result areas* (WRAs). (Note, WRA also stands for Wolf Rinke Associates.) These are the make-or-break activities, the ones that will cost you your job if you do not complete them. If you have developed your humongous overarching goal (HOG), it is very likely one of your top three. So write these down. In fact, some of my clients keep them right on their PDA or laptop. (If you don't know what your WRAs are, stay with me, and I'll help you to get a handle on them shortly.)

How to Get the Most Out of Every 24 Hours

Step 1. Record Your Time

Keep a time log for at least three to five days—three days if your work is somewhat repetitive and five days if it is not. It is important that this be done as soon as possible after you have completed a particular task or activity instead of from memory at the end of the day. An easy way to do this is to record your activities on your calendar, electronic or paper, in half-hour increments.

Step 2. Analyze Your Time Expenditures

Now take a look at each task listed in your calendar and ask yourself several diagnostic questions. The first and most important is: "What would happen if I did not do this task or activity at all?"

If the answer is *nothing*, stop doing it. (This will save you more time than you can begin to imagine.) If you are not sure, figure out how it originated. Is it something a regulatory agency requires, or is it something that your boss told you to do or a customer suggested? Go back and find out whether the originator wants you to continue or if it is still required in a current regulation. Note the words are *required* and *current*, not *nice to have* or *because we always have done it that way* or even *it is in one of our standard operating procedures.*

If you can't figure out how the practice originated and you don't see any positive impact on the bottom line, quit doing it, but be sure to track it by making a note in your computerized tickler file that will remind you to check on your decision. Let's say that it is a policy in your department that you meet with your management team twice a week. You have a very competent team and an outstanding team leader who is quite capable of conducting the meeting. When you check with your team leader, you can find no information that requires you to personally conduct this meeting. In this case you might make the decision to let your team leader handle the meetings. Make a note on the calendar to check on your decision in about two months. If your boss hasn't said anything and your employees are still as productive as always, then you have made yourself some discretionary time.

The next question is: "Will this activity move me closer to the attainment of my top three critical priorities?" If the answer is no, don't do it, unless, of course, you boss asked you. In that case it is a critical priority, unless you talk your boss out of it. If the answer is yes, go to step 3.

The next question is: "Can this be delegated?" If the answer is yes, ask for a volunteer. If no one volunteers, assign it to someone who will grow from doing it. If the answer is no, keep reading to find out what to do with it.

Step 3. Look for Time Patterns

Next, look for patterns in your use of time so that you can figure out how you can chunk your time. Let's assume that your three- to five-day time record reveals that you are faced with constant interruptions from the telephone, employees, and salespeople, as well as a wide variety of administrative functions such as signing requisitions and other documents. These patterns will provide you with an opportunity to stretch your time rubber band by collapsing like activities. For example, you might establish a policy that you will only talk to vendors and answer other routine calls during specified times of the day, let's say from 2 to 3 P.M., or you answer e-mails only once a day—ideally just before you go home—that way you will spend less time on it.

To address the constant interruptions, you may want to abolish the sacrosanct open-door policy. You would be much better served by scheduling a large chunk of your time to practicing management by walking around (MBWA). In the long run, this will be help you to be more responsive to the needs of your team members and will aid in your keeping in touch with them. Other meetings should be handled by appointment only, which also should be done only during certain periods of the day or the week. By setting time aside in this fashion, you will find that you are much more attentive and listen more actively. Let me hasten to say at this point that I am talking only about routine matters. Obviously, you must still take care of the *true* emergencies.

Step 4. Categorize Your Tasks

Your next step is to categorize your time to figure out whether you spend most of your time on the many trivial tasks—let's call them the "irrelevant many"—or on the important tasks—let's call them the WRAs. To make this more meaningful, it is important for you to internalize the Pareto principle, better known as the *80-20 rule*. Vilfredo Pareto was an Italian economist who maintained that 80 percent of the important results are accomplished in 20 percent of the time. This phenomenon exists because work falls into two major categories—WRAs and the irrelevant many. The irrelevant many are all the things that have to be done to keep the operation going. They include such things as filling out forms, attending meetings, answering most e-mails, and so on. Pareto estimated that these activities will use up about 80 percent of your time. The time that you have left, about 20 percent, is the time that you will devote to the WRAs. These are the things that will decide whether you or your company will be a leader in the industry and whether you will be promoted or get a bonus. They include such things as taking care of customers, developing team members, and achieving the HOG.

What makes this so powerful is that if you are able to allocate just a little more time to the WRAs, you will realize massive productivity increases. For example, by allocating just 1 percent more of your time to the WRAs, you will realize an increase of 4 percent in the WRAs. This represents a 400 percent return on your time investment, which is the kind of result that most of us dream about. Since 1 percent is not very much, figure out what would happen to your performance and career if you could devote 4 percent more time to the WRAs. Your accomplishments certainly would achieve hyperspeed.

Step 5. Allocate Your Tasks

Now let's go back to your time record to help figure out how you can allocate more of your time to the WRAs. Tasks that you currently complete that are of short duration and simple are likely among the irrelevant many. Find a volunteer to delegate them to. If you can't delegate them, do them fast and efficiently because, no matter how well you do them, they will only provide you with a minimal payoff.

Tasks that are of short duration but are important and/or complex in nature are probably WRAs. Consider delegating these to team members on whom you can count to get the job done or who have the potential and need the experience to maximize their potential. If you have no one like that on your team, do these yourself. Be sure to group a number of these together so that you can do more than one while in this thinking mode.

Tasks that you are currently doing that take a long time and are complex are probably WRAs—the ones that may have the 400 percent payoff. Delegate these only to those who have a track record of being able to accomplish them effectively. If you have no one like that, *do them yourself*. Allocate as much time as possible to these, and if you have more than you can handle—which is likely—prioritize them to be sure to do those with the highest potential payoff first. To increase your effectiveness, you will need a large chunk of time and as quiet a location as you can find. In other words, you will need to create a "time island"—a time and place where you will not be disturbed except for true emergencies. Be sure to work on these during a time of the day when you are at your best. Subdivide the project into smaller self-contained components, and work on one component at a time until it is done so that you have a sense of accomplishment each time you finish a component.

Work From a To-Do List Every Day

"If you want to eat an elephant, you have to take one bite at a time." I'm sure that your job is just like that proverbial elephant, and if you want to master it—instead of it mastering you—you must have a to-do list that drives your daily actions, and provides you with a sense of direction and focus. Many leaders tend to diminish their effectiveness because they simply come to work without a "roadmap" for the day. They don't ask themselves, "What three to five things can I accomplish today that will make a big difference to the bottom line?"

So, first thing in the morning or last thing before you go home, write down three to five critical tasks that you want to get done that day. During the course of the day, especially after you have been interrupted, look back at your list to make sure that you have not lulled yourself away from the critical items on your list. This takes a lot of will power because, as you well know, it is so much more comfortable to work on the irrelevant many. My strategy is to be tenacious about the top items on the list to the point that most of the time—to the chagrin of my wife—I won't call it a day until they are done.

Which strategy you use to stretch your time rubber band is not important, provided that it "forces" you to work on the WRAs and it disciplines you to finish one task before starting another. You see, how many projects you *start* doesn't count at all; the number you *finish*, even if it is only one important one, does. In fact, being busy or working long hours doesn't count either; results, especially the WRAs, do. So visualize your prioritized tasks, and work them tenaciously until they are done. Never worry about all the things you are not doing or all the things you were unable to accomplish yesterday because yesterday is gone, and all the fretting in the world won't make it come back.

Take Advantage of the Three-Minute Rule

This is the system that will enable you to stretch your time rubber band. It works! Use it as a guideline, and stay flexible. I said *guideline* because of a recent experience. One of my clients had just finished reading a current time management book and was trying to abide by the rules the author had prescribed. Proud of his success, he was telling me how he had just told someone who had called him that he would get the answer and call back so that he could continue working on a major project. Because I was in the process of writing this chapter, I asked him about the question and found out that it was a fairly simple one that probably could have been answered in a matter of minutes while the other party remained on the line. When I asked my client why he had not taken care of it right away, he said something to the effect of wanting to chunk his time so that he could concentrate on the major activities at hand.

In this case, the operation was a success, but the patient died. By the time my client finally was able to reconnect with the caller who had an easy-to-answer question, he would have used up far more time than he saved by chunking his time. In other words, the literal application of a theory seldom works unless you tailor it to yourself and to the situation and then superimpose some common sense. To help my client, I shared the *three-minute rule* with him: Once interrupted, do anything that can be completed in three minutes or less. You will find that even though it may violate one of the other rules you were taught, it will save you lots of time in the long run. The moral of this story is that you always must look at the bottom line and ask which, all things considered, is the most cost-effective strategy in the long run. Happy stretching!

Smile

All this time management stuff reminds me of a cartoon by Scott Stantis called "The Buckets." It shows a man in an office sitting in front of his computer while talking on the phone and surrounded by technology. The man is saying to himself: "I have e-mail and voice mail . . . a fax machine and an answering machine . . . two phone lines and a cellular . . . a beeper and an electronic notepad . . . a laptop and a desktop. So where's all the time I've supposedly saved?"

SMART STEPS

Starting today, cut all meeting times by 25 percent. Trust me, you will still get everything done as before.

Have all meetings that are longer than 30 minutes driven by an agenda that is time-, task-, and people-specific.

Start and stop every meeting on time. If it cannot be accomplished in the allocated time, ask for a small team to work on it and bring back recommendations to consider at a future meeting.

Starting tomorrow and continuing for three months, pick a day of the week when you commit to scrutinizing everything you do by asking: "What will happen to the bottom line if I no longer do this?" If the answer is *nothing*, quit doing it.

For the next 90 days, pick one task per week and delegate it to someone on your team.

Religiously record your time usage for the next three to five days, and then analyze it and figure out what practices you can:

Chunk or combine for greater efficiency.

Give up altogether.

Delegate to someone else on your team.

Automate or "routinize."

Scrutinize every crisis for the next 120 days, and figure out what can be done so that the crisis will not ever recur as a crisis. If you can't figure it out, get help.

Figure out which time of the day you are the most productive. Block this time out on your calendar for at least the next 21 working days so that it becomes habit. Now do your most important and longest projects—the WRAs—during this time.

Continued

Continued

If you have trouble with procrastination, take your top priority and, if it is a long project, break it down into self-contained chunks. Estimate how long it will take you to complete chunk one. Block out this time on your calendar during one of your designated productive times. Clearly mark on the calendar what is to be accomplished during this time. When the time comes, *start* and commit yourself to not doing anything else, including going home, until the designated chunk is done.

During the next six months, reduce all policies and procedures by half. Repeat this process every six months until you are down to those which are required by a regulatory agency or are used extensively. (The way you can tell the latter is to see if the pages are torn and worn. If not, they exist only for show.)

20

Don't Be Committed

The Rat Race

There are those who say life is a rat race.
Yet they want to come in first place.
So they run faster and faster
To become a fat cat.
And even if they win . . .
They're still only a rat.

—Unknown

Professor Sydney Finkelstein, author of *Why Smart Executives Fail*,[1] says that even though being committed appears to be a positive attribute—who wouldn't want a leader who is totally committed to the company—it's a handicap because these unsuccessful leaders see themselves as an extension of the company. This "private empire" mentality causes the leader to behave as if she owns the company. As a result, the leader carries out personal ambitions and takes extraordinary risks. Since there is no boundary between the leader and the company, such leaders spend the company's money as if it were their own and never quite see what the problem is when

161

they do so. A perfect example is Dennis Kozlowski of Tyco, who used corporate funds to support his own extravagant lifestyle. And he thought it was perfectly okay to do so. After all, he reasoned, the money he pulled out for his personal use was infinitesimally small compared with all the money *he* had made for Tyco. Similarly, committed leaders dedicate virtually all their time to the organization and expect everyone to do the same.

A middle manager in one of my seminars comes to mind. She took serious offense to my speaking about work-life balance and nurturing successful personal relationships. When I attempted to patch things up with her after the seminar, she let me know that the company was her life and that she had virtually no other interests outside the company. She felt that it was totally inappropriate for me to tell that "silly story about balance [see the end of this chapter] because who are you to impose your lifestyle on the rest of us." Therefore, instead of being committed, I urge you to balance your life.

How to Balance Your Life and Conquer Stress

It's no secret. Life has become too fast. Most of us are overcommitted, overwhelmed, and overinformed. In other words, most of us are just plain stressed out. Here are eight specific things you can begin to do today to reestablish balance in your life and deal more effectively with stress.

Take Control

Stress is weird. What stresses some turns others on. However, the research is rather clear: All of us feel stressed when we feel out of control. And how you feel is a perception—as opposed to reality—that you can control. In other words, you are not stressed until you tell yourself that you are stressed. To avoid feeling out of control, master your internal and external language. Use language that empowers you instead of stresses you. For example, instead of saying "I *have* to," say "I *want* to." When you *have* to do something, you become a victim. Instead of saying, "I have to go to work," say, "I want to go to work." There is only one thing you have to do, and that is to die. Everything else is a choice. Some people disagree; they say that you also have to pay taxes. No, you don't! I'm fond of saying that I want to pay my taxes because it is the lesser of the two evils. I would rather pay my taxes than go to jail. Think about it: The more taxes you pay, the more money you make. So be sure not to give your choices away.

Master the Most Powerful Stress-Control System of All Time

Change the Changeable

If something is bothering you, do something about it now. For example, if you are feeling overwhelmed, make a list of the things that are overwhelming you. Be very specific. Prioritize the list, and then start working on priority number one and so on. The simple act of doing *something* will give you a sense of being in control.

Accept the Unchangeable

There are lots of things you can do nothing about, no matter how much you fret or worry. Here are just a couple of items that come to mind: the weather, other people's actions, your skin color, your parents, where you grew up, and—the biggest one of all—the past. Accept these for what they are—and just get on with it.

Remove Yourself from the Unacceptable

For example, if you work in a "toxic" organization, find yourself a new job. And take extra care about who you hang out with. Remember: *If you sleep with dogs, you'll wake up with fleas.* So be sure to associate with positive people—people who feel that they are in control of their lives.

Make a Weekly Date with Your Significant Other

"Superwoman"—that's my beloved wife, Marcela, my partner for over 30 years— and I have a weekly date during which we pamper each other. It usually consists of a hot tub, private time, and romance. We have done this for as long as we've been married. I guess that this is why we are more in love today than the day we got married. I strongly recommend that you block out private time on your calendar and that you take it more seriously than any other appointment. After all, the only person you have the opportunity to share a life with is your spouse. Don't miss that opportunity!

Simplify Your Life

Take a look at all the things you do and have. Ask yourself what is giving you pleasure and what is giving you pain. Then begin to get rid of the things that are taking away from the quality of your life. For example, do you really need eight credit cards, or would you be better off if you had "plastic surgery"? Do you enjoy mowing your own lawn or cleaning your house? If not, hire someone else to do it. Before you acquire anything new, ask: "Is this going to make my life simpler or more complex?" Then act accordingly. For example, does buying a summer home improve the quality of your life, or does it add to your workload and to your level of perceived stress? Or would it be cheaper and more enjoyable to rent one whenever you feel like it?

Create Solitude

Unless it is absolutely essential, do *not* give your home phone number to business associates or clients. When you go on vacation, leave your beeper, cell phone, personal digital assistant (PDA), and laptop behind. If you must, call the office only once a day, and instruct the office to only get in touch with you in *true* emergencies. When at work, make it a practice to close your office door, turn the phone over to voice mail, and meditate for 20 minutes every working day. Or do what I do. Eat a very light and quick lunch, and use the rest of your time to take a brisk walk.

Exercise—Your Life Depends on It

Aerobic exercise is a great stress reducer. In addition, it extends your life. Research tells us that for every hour of aerobic exercise, your life expectancy is extended by two hours. This is a pretty good return on investment, isn't it? The key to making this work is to find something that you love to do and that you can do for the rest of your life. For me, it is jogging about three miles every other day. My wife has difficulty with her back, so she uses the ski or bicycle machine instead. On the other days we do resistance training. Sunday we rest. If at all possible, avoid exercising in the evening. Exercise cranks up your metabolic rate, energizes you, and keeps you awake, so, if possible, exercise first thing in the morning.

Sleep Well

Researchers tell us that most of us do not get enough sleep. The average person sleeps less than seven hours. To achieve peak performance, however, your body requires eight hours of sleep. Consistently sleeping less than eight hours results in lower productivity, more accidents, and more stress. According to Timothy Roehrs, director of the Henry Ford Hospital of Sleep Disorders and Research Center in Detroit, there are four strategies that will enable you to get more out of your sleep:[2]

> *Maintain a regular sleep schedule.* To get the most from your sleep, go to bed and get up at approximately the same time every day. Although this is good advice, "Superwoman" and I allow ourselves the luxury of sleeping in on Sundays. And why not? Some of the research evidence suggests that we are able to "store" some sleep.
>
> *Wind down.* Be sure to create a wind-down phase before going to sleep. What works like magic for us is television. Although I'm not a proponent of TV, I do advocate it as a tool for getting sleepy. When I'm at home, we typically read until about 9 P.M. We tape the national news and our favorite shows—that way we can skip the commercials—and then we watch until we are ready to go to bed at about 11 P.M.
>
> *Eat as early as possible.* Avoid eating before going to bed. In fact, eat your main meal as early as possible in the day. It will help you with your weight-control program, and it will help you to sleep better at night. Also be sure to avoid caffeine and alcohol late in the day.
>
> *Don't fight it.* If you find yourself unable to sleep, don't fight it. Get up, get yourself a warm glass of milk (yes, it actually does work), watch a boring TV program, or read something that will calm you down. (This is how I catch up on all my professional journals.)

Make Time for Joy

Each week, block out time on your calendar for the sole purpose of doing something that gives you joy and relaxes and calms you. For me, it's being with nature, hiking, working in the garden, or mowing the lawn. For you, it might be seeing friends, getting a massage, meditating, or going to the theater with a loved one. Whatever you do, make sure that you build joy into your life.

In closing, I would like to leave you with a story that puts balance in focus.

Keep Your Life in Balance—a Wake-Up Call

Can you be too motivated, too focused, and too driven? Now that's a question you would *not* expect to hear from someone who speaks all over the world and has written extensively on the topics of motivation, focus, and achievement. In this story I would like to share a hidden aspect of motivation that I have not shared in any of my writings before. It has to do with balance. The reason that I have not shared this before is because I probably have not been the best role model when it comes to balance. Perhaps it is because I virtually started with no more than the clothes on my back and an eighth-grade education when I came to this country in 1960. Hence I've always been extremely driven and very materialistically motivated. Having fame, fortune, and "stuff" has been extremely important to me—until that fateful day in December 1997.

"Superwoman" (my wife) and I were on our way to Paris, France. Both of us were very excited, Marcela because we were going to one of our favorite cities and me because I would have the privilege to speak to a large group of managers from 19 different countries whom I wanted to greet in their own language. We had an uneventful trip until we got to France, when we noticed that we were in a holding pattern. After about 20 minutes the pilot calmly advised us that the indicator light for the landing gear was not working and that he and his copilot were trying to diagnose the problem. About 30 minutes later the pilot told us that there was nothing wrong with the indicator light, which meant that either the landing gear was not extended or had not locked in. "We will now," he continued, "fly over the tower so that they can make a visual inspection." After doing that twice, the pilot advised us that the landing gear appeared to be extended, so we must assume that the gear was *not* locked in. After what seemed like an eternal pause, the captain got on the intercom and said, "Ladies and gentlemen, the flight attendants will now provide you with emergency landing instructions. I know that you've heard these many times before, but this time it's different. This time I'm going to ask you to pay very close attention because this time it's for real because we will have to make an emergency landing at the Charles de Gaulle International airport." He also told us that the airport had been closed and that emergency equipment would be standing by. The flight attendants very calmly and professionally instructed us to get rid of all sharp objects, clear all isles, and put everything in the overhead bins. They also had us practice the emergency landing position—putting our head between our arms, leaning forward, and bracing ourselves against the seat in front of us.

After more than two hours, the captain finally began his descent, and everyone quietly assumed the emergency landing position on his command. What occurred to me during those eternal two hours is that at no time did I say to myself: "I wish I had worked harder, I wish I had spoken more often, I wish I had done more publicity to get more fame, I wish I had made more money, I wish I had bought more stuff." Instead, I thought about my *relationships*—my relationship with my wife and what else I could have done to love her even more, my relationship with my daughters and how they would cope without us, my relationship with my parents and why I had not told them how much I love them more often, my relationships with my friends and why I had not told them more often just how much they mean to me, and my relationship with my team members and why I had not told them more often how much I appreciate all they do.

What I learned from all this is what is *really important*: It's not money, not fame, not stuff—but relationships. Of course, being a keynote motivational speaker, I also thought, "If you make it out of this alive, you'll have one heck of a story to tell."

After the captain gave the command to assume the emergency position, he landed the plane so softly that we did not even know that we had landed, right between rows of fire engines. As you can imagine, the trip concluded with the loudest round of applause, cheers, and joy I have ever heard on any flight.

Take Action

Back to the original question: Can you be too motivated, too focused, and too driven? *Yes*—too motivated, too focused, and too driven accumulating fame, fortune, and stuff! No—when it comes to building and nurturing your relationships. So make time for the loved ones in your life—your spouse, your children, your parents, and your friends. They are more important than what you do at work. They are your safety blankets, your behind-the-scenes team—the team that allows you to do what you do at work with excellence. Without them, you would not be where you are today. So pick up the phone right now and tell those who do not live with you just how much you love and appreciate them. And be sure to hug your spouse and children who reside with you *tonight!* Give them *unconditional* love by telling them how proud you are to be their spouse or parent. Then give them a big hug and loving kisses. No, don't wait until tomorrow—do it tonight when you get home.

Now take another big chunk of energy and time and spend it on the relationship with your team members. After all, they are responsible for 85 percent of your success. How well have your nurtured those relationships? Don't be like some of the executives I coach and delude yourself. Instead, be tough with yourself. Grab your calendar and look at the last five working days. How much of your time did you dedicate to nurturing the relationships with your team members? I don't mean how much time have you spent telling them what to do. I'm talking about how much time have you spent talking *with* them—not at them? Talking with them about their personal concerns, their spouses, their children, their aging parents, and the many challenges they face? Being there for them with compassion, assistance, and time off when they have personal challenges, such as a sick child, an aging parent, or even worse, a death in the family. Here is an important realization for you to take advantage of: When the "yogurt" hits the fan, your team members will *not* do it for the organization. However, they may do it for you. How well have you treated them lately?

Be sure to keep your life in balance, and don't forget to mark out time on your calendar for spending positive energy and quality time on the *real important stuff in your life—your relationships.*

Smile

The irony of the rat race explained: On a bright and sunny day a fishing boat docked in an idyllic Greek village shortly after noon. An American tourist, who was admiring the modest catch, complimented the Greek fisherman on the quality of his fish and asked how long it took him to catch them.

"A couple of hours," answered the fisherman.

"But then, why didn't you stay out longer and catch more?" asked the American.

The fisherman explained that his small catch was sufficient to meet his needs and those of his family.

The American asked, "But what do you do with the rest of your time?"

"I sleep late, fish a little, play with my children, and take a siesta with my wife. In the evenings I go into the village to see my friends, drink a few glasses of wine, and sing a few songs. I have a full life."

The American interrupted, "I have a business degree from Wharton, and I can help you become very successful! You should get started earlier and fish longer every day. You can then sell the extra fish to a middleman. With the extra income, you can buy a bigger boat, which will then enable you to catch even more fish. With the extra money from the sale of the fish, you can buy a second boat and a third and so on until you have an entire fleet of fishing boats. At that point you can negotiate directly with the processing plants and possibly even open your own plant. You can then leave this little village and move to Athens or even San Francisco! From there you can direct your huge enterprise."

"How long would that take?" asked the Greek.

"Fifteen to maybe 20 years," replied the American.

"And after that?"

"Afterwards? That's when it gets really interesting," answered the American, laughing. "When your business gets really big, you can expand on a global scale. At that point you would be able to go public, start selling stocks, and make millions maybe even billions!"

"Millions or even billions? And what would I do after that?" asked the fisherman.

"After that you'll be able to retire, live in a tiny village near the coast, sleep late, catch a few fish, play with your children, take a siesta with your wife, and spend your evenings drinking wine and singing songs, and enjoy being with your friends."

On that introspective note, I'll say *Aufwiedersehen,* which means "I will see you again," and encourage you to practice contrarian leadership *and* live a balanced and stress-free life.

SMART STEPS

I think you agree that this chapter has enough smart steps to keep you busy for the rest of your life. Just in case you need just a bit more help, copy the "Leadership Roadmap " that follows this chapter. It's guaranteed to help you improve your leadership effectiveness if—you know what's coming—you take action!

Leadership Roadmap

"Leadership is a journey . . . not a destination"

To travel the journey, I hereby commit to

- Make work *fun.*
- Keep life in balance.
- Listen more and talk less.
- Always do the *right* thing.
- Create desire instead of fear.
- Strive to be respected—not liked.
- Encourage different points of view.
- Treat *every* employee like a volunteer.
- Live our mission, vision, and core values.
- Lead by appreciation instead of by exception.
- Display an irrational sense of hope and courage.
- Treat health and time with reverence and respect.
- Help people become more than they think is possible.
- Surround myself with people who are smarter than I am.
- Align daily efforts with a Humongous Overarching Goal (HOG).
- Look at what others are doing and have the guts to do something different.
- Focus more on employee and customer satisfaction and less on the "bottom line."
- Treat all team members as if they are the most important people in the world.
- Invest in team members so they can become the best they can be.
- Love people the way they are, not the way they ought to be.
- Trust all people all the time until *they* prove me wrong.
- Tell team members more than they want to know.
- Enable team members to build on their strengths.
- Push decision making down to the lowest level.
- Focus on the long term instead of the urgent.
- Speak from the heart, not from the head.
- Catch others doing things *almost right.*
- Exceed customers' expectations.
- Be humble, kind, and generous.
- Create desire instead of fear.
- Ask more and assign less.
- Nurture relationships.
- Celebrate often.

Remember: 85 percent of your success comes from your team members! So begin right now to treat them accordingly.

Copied with permission from W. J. Rinke, *Don't Oil the Squeaky Wheel and 19 Other Contrarian Ways to Improve Your Leadership Effectiveness* (New York: McGraw-Hill, 2004). Dr. Rinke is an internationally recognized keynote speaker, seminar leader, management consultant, executive coach, and author dedicated to helping organizations and individuals achieve dramatic improvements in performance, productivity, and profitability. To find out how you can achieve "howling" success, simply "Cry WOLF"—Wolf Rinke Associates, Inc., P. O. Box 350, Clarksville, MD 21029; phone: 800-828-WOLF; e-mail: *WolfRinke@aol.com,* or visit his Web site at *www.WolfRinke.com.*

Notes

Chapter 1
1. F. Sala, "Laughing All the Way to the Bank," *Harvard Business Review* 81(9):16, 2003. Also see www.haygroup.com/humor.

Chapter 2
1. N. Nohria, W. Joyce, and B. Roberson, "What Really Works," *Harvard Business Review* 81(7):43, 2003.
2. W. J. Rinke, *Winning Management: 6 Fail-Safe Strategies for Building High-Performance Organizations* (Clarksville, MD: Achievement Publishers, 1997).
3. Nohria et al., "What Really Works," pp. 43–52.
4. *Ibid.*, p. 44.
5. *www.gallup.com/management/Q12_system.asp.*

Chapter 3
1. W. J. Rinke, *Make It a Winning Life: Success Strategies for Life, Love and Business* (Clarksville, MD: Achievement Publishers, 1992); D. Goleman, *Emotional Intelligence: Why It Can Matter More than IQ* (New York: Bantam Books, 1995); and D. Goleman, R. Boyatzis, and A. McKee, *Primal Leadership: Realizing the Power of Emotional Intelligence* (Boston: Harvard Business School Press, 2002).
2. M. E. P. Seligman, *Authentic Happiness: Using the New Positive Psychology to Realize Your Potential for Lasting Fulfillment* (New York: Free Press, 2002); M. E. Seligman, *Learned Optimism: How to Change Your Mind and Your Life* (New York: Pocket Books, 1998); additional information available at *www.positivepsychology.org*; W. J. Rinke, *Make It a Winning Life: Success Strategies for Life, Love and Business* (Clarksville, MD : Achievement Publishers, 1992), Chap. 8.
3. Rinke, *Make It a Winning Life*, Chap. 7.

4. For specifics, see my article of the same title at *www.WolfRinke.com.*
5. E. Sullivan, *The Concise Book of Lying* (New York: Picador, 2002).

Chapter 4
1. D. Goleman, "Leadership that Gets Results," *Harvard Business Review* 78(2):78–90, 2000.
2. *Ibid.*
3. Available from HRD Press, Amherst, MA; *www.hrdpress.com.*

Chapter 5
1. R. Maurer, *Beyond the Wall of Resistance* (Austin, TX: Bard Press, 1996).
2. L. C. Thurow, "To End Quality Control Disaster, Japan Must Acknowledge Errors," *Boston Globe*, October 3, 2000.

Chapter 6
1. GE 2000 Annual Report, p. 6.
2. W. H. Peace, "The Hard Work of Being a Soft Manger," *Harvard Business Review* 79(11):99–104, 2001.
3. *Ibid.*, p. 104.
4. R. Cialdini, *Influence: Science and Practice*, 4th ed. (Boston: Pearson Allyn & Bacon, 2001); also see *www.influenceatwork.com.*
5. M. Bazerman, *Judgment in Managerial Decision Making*, 4th ed. (New York: Wiley, 1998).
6. R. Cialdini, "Harnessing the Science of Persuasion," *Harvard Business Review* 79(9):72–79, 2001.
7. M. E. Seligman, *Learned Optimism: How to Change Your Mind and Your Life* (New York: Pocket Books, 1998).

Chapter 7
1. *http://www.ethics.org/releases/nr_20030521_nbes.html*; accessed August 27, 2003.
2. S. Finkelstein, *Why Smart Executives Fail: And What You Can Learn from Their Mistakes* (New York: Portfolio, 2003); and S. Finkelstein, "7 Habits of Spectacularly Unsuccessful Executives," *Fast Company* (July):84–89, 2003.
3. J. Collins, *Good to Great: Why Some Companies Make the Leap . . . and Others Don't* (New York: HarperCollins, 2002); and J. Collins and J. I. Porras, *Built to Last: Successful Habits of Visionary Companies* (New York: Harper Business, 2002).
4. J. Smith, "Mistakes of NASA Toted Up," *The Washington Post*, July 13, 2003, pp. A1, A17.
5. R. Charan and J. Useem, "Why Companies Fail," *Fortune*, May 27, 2002, pp. 50–62.
6. J. P. Schuster and J. Carpenter, *The Power of Open-Book Management: Releasing the True Potential of People's Minds, Hearts, and Hands* (New York: Wiley, 1996).

Chapter 9
1. N. Hernandez, "Embattled Naval Academy Chief Resigns," *Washington Post*, June 5, 2003, pp. A1, A21.
2. Walker Information, *www.walkerinfo.com*; accessed May 7, 2003.
3. D. Wessel, "The Hidden Cost of Labor Strife," *Wall Street Journal*, January 10, 2002, p. A1.
4. *http://www.gallup.com/solutions/Q12_system.asp* shows you how to use the Gallup Employee Satisfaction Survey referred to as Q12.

Chapter 10

1. F. Vogelstein, "Mighty Amazon," *Fortune,* May 26, 2003, pp. 60–74.
2. D. Madson, "Gearing up at REI," *Harvard Business Review* 81(5):20–21, 2003
3. J. Huey, "The Jack and Herb Show," *Fortune,* January 11, 1999, p. 23.
4. Madsen, "Gearing Up at REI," *op. cit.,* p. 20.
5. R. Levering and M. Moskowitz, "100 Best Companies to Work For," *Fortune,* January 20, 2003, p. 128.
6. W. J. Rinke, *Make It a Winning Life: Success Strategies for Life, Love and Business* (Clarksville, MD: Achievement Publishers, 1992).

Chapter 11

1. Success Profiles, Inc., *www.successprofiles.com;* accessed June 4, 2003.
2. P. Lucas and M. Overfelt, "The Great American Company, Johnson & Johnson," *Fortune Small Business,* April 2003, pp. 91–93.
3. J. Collins, "The Ten Greatest CEO's of All Time," *Fortune,* July 21, 2003, p. 62.
4. *http://www.jnj.com/our_company/our_credo_history/index.htm;jsessionid=0VS0GMB33QRMGCQPCB3SU0A;* accessed August 6, 2003.
5. B. Broadway, "Good for the Soul—and the Bottom Line," *Washington Post,* August 19, 2001, pp. A1, A6.
6. W. J. Rinke, *Winning Management: 6 Fail-Safe Strategies for Building High-Performance Organizations* (Clarksville, MD: Achievement Publishers, 1997).
7. B. Morris, "What a Life," *Fortune,* October 6, 2003, pp. 50–62.
8. J. Collins, "Turning Goals into Results: The Power of Catalytic Mechanisms," *Harvard Business Review* 77(4):71-82, 1999.

Chapter 12

1. "Fortune 500," *Fortune,* April 14, 2003, p. F-1.
2. I. Morgan and J. Rao, "Aligning Service Strategy through Super-Measure Management," *Academy of Management Executive* 16(4):121–131, 2002.

Chapter 13

1. S. Shellenbarger, "Workplace Upheavals Seem to Be Eroding Employees' Trust," *Wall Street Journal,* June 21, 2000, p. B1.
2. *Ibid.*

Chapter 15

1. D. Madsen, "Gearing Up at REI" *Harvard Business Review* 81(5): 20-21.
2. R. McKee, "Storytelling That Moves People," *Harvard Business Review* 81(6):51–55, 2003.
3. B. Nelson and K. H. Blanchard, *1001 Ways to Reward Employees* (New York: Workman, 1994).

Chapter 16

1. "Disengaged at Work?" *Wall Street Journal,* March 13, 2001, p. A1.
2. *Ibid.*
3. P. Hemp, "My Week as a Room-Service Waiter at the Ritz," *Harvard Business Review* 80(6):56, 2002

Chapter 17

1. N. G. Carr, "The Economics of Customer Satisfaction," *Harvard Business Review* 77(2):15–18, 1999.
2. *Ibid.*, p. 18.
3. J. L. Heskett, T.O. Jones, and G.W. Loveman, "Putting the Service-Profit Chain to Work," *Harvard Business Review* 72(2):165, 1994.

Chapter 18

1. W. J. Rinke, *Winning Management: 6 Fail-Safe Strategies for Building High-Performance Organizations* (Clarksville, MD: Achievement Publishers, 1997).
2. "Report 2002: Training for the Next Economy," *http://www.astd.org/virtual_community/research/pdf/SOIR2002_Training_summary.pdf.pdf*; accessed August 12, 2003.
3. Rinke, *Winning Management.*
4. "Business Week, Annual Pay Surveys," *http://www.aflcio.org/corporateamerica/pay-watch/pay/index.cfm*; accessed September 15, 2003.
5. J. Useem, "Have They No Shame?" *Fortune*, April 28, 2003, p. 58.
6. Ibid., p. 64.
7. K. Alexander, "US Airways CEO Talks Shop," *Washington Post*, April 4, 2003, pp. E1, E6.
8. "Getting Fired Is the Best Thing That Can Happen to You," *www.WolfRinke.com.*
9. J. Collins, "Turning Goals into Results: The Power of Catalytic Mechanisms," *Harvard Business Review* 77(4):71–82, 1999.
10. M. Benjamin and J. Perry, "The New Job Reality," *U.S. News & World Report*, August 11, 2003, pp. 24–29.

Chapter 19

1. W. J. Rinke, *Time Management: How to Stretch the Time Rubber Band*, 2d ed. (Clarksville, MD: Wolf Rinke Associates, 2003).

Chapter 20

1. S. Finkelstein, *Why Smart Executives Fail: And What You Can Learn from Their Mistakes* (New York: Portfolio, 2003).
2. The National Sleep Foundation, *www.sleep-foundation.org*; accessed July 9, 2002.

Index

What Do You Think About This Book?

This is your opportunity to let me know what you think of this book. You can even become an expert contributor. Please answer the following questions in enough detail so that I have a clear idea of what, why, when, where, and how something did or did not work for you. If I incorporate your input in the next edition or in another book, I will send you a personalized copy of the book absolutely *free*.

Wolf:

The strategies you described in Chapter _____ on pages _____ worked for me.

This is how I applied them:

These are the results I achieved:

The strategies you described in Chapter _____ on pages _____ did not work for me.

This is how I tried to use them:

These are the results I achieved:

This is how I fixed it:

The following pages describe a personal experience related to the topic of your book. Please feel free to use it as you wish.

Your signature: _____

Today's date: _____

Your name, complete mailing address, and telephone number (please print):

Mail to: Wolf J. Rinke, Ph.D.
            P. O. Box 350
            Clarksville, MD 21029
            E-mail: *WolfRinke@aol.com*
            www.WolfRinke.com

Thanks in advance for taking the time to provide me with your feedback